Rethinking Income and Money

Geoff Crocker

Rethinking Income and Money

Incorporating Technology into Economic Theory

palgrave macmillan

Geoff Crocker
Bristol, UK

ISBN 978-3-031-77781-3   ISBN 978-3-031-77782-0 (eBook)
https://doi.org/10.1007/978-3-031-77782-0

© The Editor(s) (if applicable) and The Author(s), under exclusive license to Springer Nature Switzerland AG 2025

This work is subject to copyright. All rights are solely and exclusively licensed by the Publisher, whether the whole or part of the material is concerned, specifically the rights of translation, reprinting, reuse of illustrations, recitation, broadcasting, reproduction on microfilms or in any other physical way, and transmission or information storage and retrieval, electronic adaptation, computer software, or by similar or dissimilar methodology now known or hereafter developed.

The use of general descriptive names, registered names, trademarks, service marks, etc. in this publication does not imply, even in the absence of a specific statement, that such names are exempt from the relevant protective laws and regulations and therefore free for general use.

The publisher, the authors and the editors are safe to assume that the advice and information in this book are believed to be true and accurate at the date of publication. Neither the publisher nor the authors or the editors give a warranty, expressed or implied, with respect to the material contained herein or for any errors or omissions that may have been made. The publisher remains neutral with regard to jurisdictional claims in published maps and institutional affiliations.

Cover illustration: © John Rawsterne/patternhead.com

This Palgrave Macmillan imprint is published by the registered company Springer Nature Switzerland AG

The registered company address is: Gewerbestrasse 11, 6330 Cham, Switzerland

If disposing of this product, please recycle the paper.

Summary

Whilst contemporary economies succeed in supplying an increasingly wide range of products and services, and in raising the average standard of living, they also suffer from significant dysfunctionalities which include

- economic crisis
- pervasive debt
- continuous austerity
- extensive poverty
- specifically in-work poverty
- low pay
- burgeoning inequality
- extensive environmental damage.

Of these, this book focuses on the twin urgent need to

- ensure adequate sustainable household income
- reduce debt in the economy.

This focus drives the need to rethink

- **income**, its source and sustainability
- **money**, its nature as debt

and to redefine income and money in a revised economic paradigm. Specifically, the claim is that, due to technological automation, employment cannot provide adequate income for all, and that funding of government expenditure by debt is unsustainable.

The book also explores ways to incorporate **technology** into economic theory, both because

- the economy critically depends on technology
    - to create products and services
    - to automate for cost-effective mass production, distribution, and transactions
    - to reduce real price, hence raising standards of living
- technology has significance for the understanding of income and money.

The analysis suggests that economic theory has failed to adequately explain the economy. This leads to weaknesses in economic modelling to predict or simulate the economy, and in economic policy to manage the economy and deliver desired outcomes. The book therefore includes a critique of economic theory as an appendix.

The main policy proposals resulting from the analysis are

- the impact of technological automation in reducing the income of low-income households requires a hybrid policy, incorporating a small universal income, and substantially reduced conditionality of increased targeted welfare income
- some direct money financing of government expenditure should be validated.

Contents

A Personal Journey	1
On Income	7
On Money	43
On Technology	71
On Policy	95
On Theory—An Appendix	97
Index	129

LIST OF FIGURES

On Income

Fig. 1	Mean and median UK household disposable income 1977–2022 (2022 prices) (*Source* ONS Households Disposable Income and Expenditure dataset: www.ons.gov.uk/peoplepopulationandcommunity/ personalandhouseholdfinances/incomeandwealth/ datasets/householddisposableincomeandinequality Table 1: Timeseries of mean and median equivalised household disposable income, 1977–2021/22, UK [2021/22 prices])	10
Fig. 2	Median disposable household income by income quintile 1977–2022 (2022 prices) (*Source* ONS Households Disposable Income and Expenditure dataset: www.ons.gov.uk/peoplepopulationandcommunity/ personalandhouseholdfinances/incomeandwealth/ datasets/householddisposableincomeandinequality Table 2: Timeseries of median equivalised disposable household income of individuals by income quintile, 1977–2021/22, UK [2021/22 prices])	11

x LIST OF FIGURES

Fig. 3 Share of UK national household disposable income by income quintile 2022 (*Source* ONS Households Disposable Income and Expenditure dataset: www.ons.gov.uk/peoplepopulationandcommunity/personalandhouseholdfinances/incomeandwealth/datasets/householddisposableincomeandinequality Table 4: Percentage shares of equivalised household income and Gini coefficients, ALL individuals, RETIRED individuals and NON-RETIRED individuals, 2021/22, UK) 12

Fig. 4 Mean disposable UK household income of working families with children by quintile 1977–2022 (2022 prices) (*Source* ONS Households Disposable Income and Expenditure dataset: www.ons.gov.uk/peoplepopulationandcommunity/personalandhouseholdfinances/incomeandwealth/datasets/householddisposableincomeandinequality Table 5: Mean equivalised disposable household income by quintile for all individuals in non-retired households with children, 1977–2021/22, UK [2021/22 prices]) 13

Fig. 5 Individual income and benefits by income quintile (*Source* ONS Households Disposable Income and Expenditure dataset: www.ons.gov.uk/peoplepopulationandcommunity/personalandhouseholdfinances/incomeandwealth/datasets/householddisposableincomeandinequality Table 12: Summary of the effects of taxes and benefits on ALL individuals by quintile group, 2021/22, UK) 14

Fig. 6 Individual gross income, tax, and disposable income by income quintile 2022 (*Source* ONS Households Disposable Income and Expenditure dataset: www.ons.gov.uk/peoplepopulationandcommunity/personalandhouseholdfinances/incomeandwealth/datasets/householddisposableincomeandinequality Table 12: Summary of the effects of taxes and benefits on ALL individuals by quintile group, 2021/22, UK) 15

Fig. 7	Sources of gross household income by quintile 2022 (*Source* ONS Households Disposable Income and Expenditure dataset: www.ons.gov.uk/peoplepopulationandcommunity/ personalandhouseholdfinances/incomeandwealth/ datasets/householddisposableincomeandinequality Table 13: Average household incomes, taxes and benefits of ALL individuals by quintile group, 2021/22, UK)	16
Fig. 8	Household income deductions by quintile 2022 (*Source* ONS Households Disposable Income and Expenditure dataset: www.ons.gov.uk/peoplepopulationandcommunity/ personalandhouseholdfinances/incomeandwealth/ datasets/householddisposableincomeandinequality Table 13: Average household incomes, taxes and benefits of ALL individuals by quintile group, 2021/22, UK)	17
Fig. 9	% sources of UK household income 1977–2002 (*Source* ONS Households Disposable Income and Expenditure dataset: www.ons.gov.uk/peoplepopulationandcommunity/ personalandhouseholdfinances/incomeandwealth/ datasets/householddisposableincomeandinequality Table 28: Income and source of income for all UK households, 1977 to 2021/22 [2021/22 prices])	18
Fig. 10	% households with property and financial debt by income decile 2018–2020 (*Source* ONS Household Debt: Wealth in Great Britain, July 2010 to June 2016 / April 2014 to March 2020 www.ons.gov.uk/peoplepopulationandcommunity/ personalandhouseholdfinances/incomeandwealth/ datasets/householddebtwealthingreatbritain Table 7.4 Percentage of households with household debt and summary statistics by components, by total household net equivalised income decile1,2,3)	19
Fig. 11	Net acquisition of loans as a % of GDP (Blue Book—UK national accounts) (*Source* ONS UK National Accounts, The Blue Book: 2023 www.ons.gov.uk/releases/ uknationalaccountsthebluebook2023)	20

xii   LIST OF FIGURES

Fig. 12	UK gross disposable income (*Source* ONS Households Disposable Income and Expenditure dataset: www.ons.gov.uk/peoplepopulationandcommunity/ personalandhouseholdfinances/incomeandwealth/ datasets/householddisposableincomeandinequality Table 1 UK household disposable income 1977–2022 [2022 prices])	21
Fig. 12a	Consumption in excess of income per head (*Source* ONS Household final consumption expenditure: National concept CVM SA—£m www.ons.gov.uk/economy/ nationalaccounts/satelliteaccounts/timeseries/abjr/pn2)	22
Fig. 13	Correlation between equity withdrawals and the difference between GDP and consumption (*Source* Dr Joe Chrisp 'The political economy of household debt, disposable income and consumption' Institute for Policy Research at the University of Bath, February 2024, Fig. 16 Reproduced with permission www.bath.ac.uk/publications/ the-political-economy-of-household-debt-disposable-income-and-consumption)	23
Fig. 14	Gross disposable income and net acquired debt in Anglophone countries (*Source* Dr Joe Chrisp 'The political economy of household debt, disposable income and consumption' Institute for Policy Research at the University of Bath, February 2024, Fig. 25 Reproduced with permission www.bath.ac.uk/publications/ the-political-economy-of-household-debt-disposable-income-and-consumption)	24
Fig. 15	Household debt as % GDP in OECD countries (*Source* Dr Joe Chrisp 'The political economy of household debt, disposable income and consumption' Institute for Policy Research at the University of Bath, February 2024, Fig. 1 Reproduced with permission www.bath.ac.uk/publications/ the-political-economy-of-household-debt-disposable-income-and-consumption)	25

LIST OF FIGURES   xiii

Fig. 16	Household debt in the UK as % GDP (*Source* Dr Joe Chrisp 'The political economy of household debt, disposable income and consumption' Institute for Policy Research at the University of Bath, February 2024, Fig. 2 Reproduced with permission www.bath.ac.uk/publications/the-political-economy-of-household-debt-disposable-income-and-consumption)	26
Fig. 17	Household debt as % GDP (*Source* Dr Joe Chrisp 'The political economy of household debt, disposable income and consumption' Institute for Policy Research at the University of Bath, February 2024, Fig. 3 Reproduced with permission www.bath.ac.uk/publications/the-political-economy-of-household-debt-disposable-income-and-consumption)	27
Fig. 18	Aggregate labour share average of OECD countries (*Source* Dr Joe Chrisp 'The political economy of household debt, disposable income and consumption' Institute for Policy Research at the University of Bath, February 2024, Fig. 4 Reproduced with permission www.bath.ac.uk/publications/the-political-economy-of-household-debt-disposable-income-and-consumption)	28
Fig. 19	UK labour share of income (*Source* ONS Labour share of income: Whole economy SA: percentage: UK www.ons.gov.uk/employmentandlabourmarket/peopleinwork/labourproductivity/timeseries/fzln/ucst)	31
Fig. 20	Real growth in minimum wage OECD countries (*Source* GOV.UK https://assets.publishing.service.gov.uk/media/5c9e3e4e40f0b625e1cbd852/20_years_of_the_National_Minimum_Wage_-_data.xlsx Slide 11 [2]: Change in real minimum wages in OECD countries)	34
Fig. 21	Proportion of employment by pay rate (*Source* ONS Low and high pay in the UK: 2023 https://www.ons.gov.uk/employmentandlabourmarket/peopleinwork/earningsandworkinghours/bulletins/lowandhighpayuk/2023 Fig. 1)	35

xiv   LIST OF FIGURES

Fig. 22   Welfare benefits as % household income (*Source* ONS Households Disposable Income and Expenditure dataset: www.ons.gov.uk/peoplepopulationandcommunity/personalandhouseholdfinances/incomeandwealth/datasets/householddisposableincomeandinequality Table 28: Income and source of income for all UK households, 1977 to 2021/22 [2021/22 prices])   36

Fig. 23   Average household gross wage (*Source* ONS Households Disposable Income and Expenditure dataset: www.ons.gov.uk/peoplepopulationandcommunity/personalandhouseholdfinances/incomeandwealth/datasets/householddisposableincomeandinequality Table 28: Income and source of income for all UK households, 1977 to 2021/22 [2021/22 prices])   37

Fig. 24   Average household gross benefits (*Source* ONS Households Disposable Income and Expenditure dataset: www.ons.gov.uk/peoplepopulationandcommunity/personalandhouseholdfinances/incomeandwealth/datasets/householddisposableincomeandinequality Table 28: Income and source of income for all UK households, 1977 to 2021/22 [2021/22 prices])   38

On Money

Fig. 1   Debt/GDP for selected countries 1950–2022 *Source* IMF Central Government Debt,www.imf.org/external/datamapper/CG_DEBT_GDP@GDD/CHN/FRA/DEU/ITA/JPN/GBR/USA   53

Fig. 2   Debt/GDP ratios OECD countries 2022 *Source* OECD General Government Debt www.oecd.org/en/data/indicators/general-government-debt.html   54

Fig. 3   Debt funding of government expenditure   64

Fig. 4   Quantitative Easing after debt funding of government expenditure   64

Fig. 5   Proposals for central bank interest-free reserves   65

Fig. 6   Direct money financing of government expenditure   65

List of Tables

On Income

Table 1	Income structure by group	29
Table 2	Cumulative gross cost of lower conditionality of targeted welfare benefits	40

On Technology

Table 1	The techno-economic process	74

A Personal Journey

Abstract How my thinking has evolved.

Keywords Economic theory · Automation · Labour income · Money · Debt · Austerity

This book has evolved from a process of observation, hypothesis, debate and research. After graduating in economics, when Axel Leijonhufvud's 'On Keynesian Economics and the Economics of Keynes'[1] was a major resource, my professional career focussed on technology strategy development for a wide range of clients, harnessing industry sector economics, the theory of the firm, and market dynamics. A myriad of case studies demonstrated the vibrant impact of technology on the economy.

In an earlier book,[2] I explore the nature of technology, in terms of both philosophy and economics. The question from philosophy is to understand the balance between human agency and an autonomous technology process. Can we manage technology, or does it effectively lead us? A leading question from economics is whether technology reduces labour income in the economy, and may lead to deficient aggregate demand in the Keynesian sense. If so, this may prove relevant as a possible structural explanation of the 2007/8 economic crisis, and to the perpetuation of poverty in technologically advanced economies.

As the late Nobel laureate economist Robert Solow commented, with burgeoning production from advanced technologies 'the wage will absorb only a small fraction of all that output. The rest will be imputed to capital…the extreme case of this is the common scare about universal robots: labour is no longer needed at all. How will we then live? The ownership of capital will have to be democratised…(needing) some form of universal dividend…Not much thought has been given to this problem'.[3] Following Solow's insight, in a second book,[4] I analyse the case for a universal basic income to supplement aggregate demand and provide adequate income universally.

Subsequent research at the Institute for Policy Research at the University of Bath UK,[5] confirming the results of a 2013 paper by Karabarbounis and Neiman[6] concluded that technology, when measured by the declining price of capital goods, can be shown to effect a reduction in the labour share in the economy. This effect most probably derives from the process of 'capital deepening' whereby a developed technology spreads more widely in the production of goods and services. During this process, economies of scale in the production of capital equipment can be expected to reduce the cost of capital goods, incentivising their further deployment, which then reduces the labour component of production, and hence the labour share in the economy. This analysis does not however cover the effects of major quantum leaps in technology paradigms, when radically innovative technologies ranging from 'Fordist' mass production, to Internet consumer transactions, to artificial intelligence, fundamentally change the structure of the economy and its outcomes.

Further research by Cambridge Econometrics UK[7] showed that injection of a basic income into the economy to correct deficient demand, and then to replace labour income lost to automation, generated a stable outcome without inflationary consequences, as demand took up excess capacity in the economy, and then incentivised investment to increase productive capacity.

This book builds on these foundations, extending and refining the argument in the light of subsequent research and debate. Inadequate unequal income, and pervasive debt, both at the household and government level, continue to characterise and constrain the economy. If measures of aggregate income don't make income inadequacy totally clear, then disaggregating income to household income quintiles certainly does. Moreover, the phenomenon of in-work poverty demonstrates that high-wage work is not a reliable source of income for all, meaning that non-labour social or 'welfare' income is needed.

The main question is then whether increased welfare income is best targeted conditionally, or granted universally. The main defects of conditionality, i.e. intrusion, humiliation, low take-up rates, and the unemployment and poverty traps resulting from high withdrawal taper rates, may be mitigated by reduced conditionality. Further research by IPR Bath[8] shows the feasibility of reduced conditionality, which leads me to a revised hybrid proposal for some universal income together with targeted welfare benefits subjected to lower conditions.

The allied questions are those of affordability, the role of money, monetary policy, and the nature of debt. Is affordability determined by what we can actually do, as Keynes famously claimed, 'anything we can actually do we can afford' (BBC radio interview April 1942),[9] or by what money we have available, as asserted by Rachel Reeves, the new 2024 UK Chancellor of the Exchequer, 'if we cannot afford it, we cannot do it'.[10] These are radically opposite claims, with radically alternative implications for economic policy and economic outcomes. Keynes's claim needs to be modified to refer to anything we can do simultaneously at any one time, as we clearly cannot do everything at once. Reeves's claim sees money, rather than real natural and human resource, as the binding constraint. The debate focusses on how much debt government can assume to fund further expenditure. The second section of this book therefore examines the nature of money and debt from their fundamentals. I differ from the school of 'Modern Monetary Theory', known as MMT, in that I claim money is not quintessentially debt, a claim which has radical implications.

Monetary policy is centrally implicated in this debate. Governments which exercised huge 'Quantitative easing' programmes to stimulate their post-crisis economies are now implementing 'quantitative tightening'. I examine the implications and consequences of these shifts in monetary policy to argue for the superiority of direct money financing of government expenditure.

A very significant restructuring of the management of the economy results from this proposal. If some part of government expenditure were to be financed by direct money financing, then the upwards spiral of government debt, which is now comparable to the level of annual GDP, would be reduced, along with the implied debt/GDP ratio, and the substantial annual financing cost of this debt. The remaining reduced government debt would be more easily affordable, and would not constrain feasible and needed government expenditure. Crucially, government debt would no longer enforce austerity with its damaging social effects.

The combined proposal for enhanced social welfare income together with some direct money financing of government expenditure would be effective in addressing the two urgent problems we face of inadequate low-quintile household incomes, and the excess of both household and government debt.

The overall question of how technology determines the economy is extremely challenging, both conceptually and in terms of data and its measurement. The third section of the book reviews the extensive recent literature on the effect of technology on employment, sets the main points from each contribution into the evolving debate, and sketches an outline for a more comprehensive model of the technology/economy interface. The challenge of managing technology has important wider implications, principally in achieving a green economy. This necessary and major thrust in economic activity will generate employment, but will still embody increased automation, generating high-skill employment incomes, but for few people. The widespread popularity of virtual online services represents a major component of output GDP which is not labour intensive in its production, and hence limits employment income.

Finally, I offer a fairly comprehensive critique of economic theory which I suggest needs radical redirection if it is to serve economic thinking and policy.

Data and analysis are taken mainly from the UK economy as a case study, with reference to wider OECD country economies' data, but I claim that the argument of the book is universally applicable. The section on technology refers more extensively to data from the US economy, but again is presented as a case study of a general phenomenon.

References
1. Axel Leijonhufvud, *On Keynesian Economics and the Economics of Keynes* (Oxford University Press, 1968).
2. Geoff Crocker, *A Managerial Philosophy of Technology* (Palgrave, 2012), available as a free download at www.philosophyoftecnology.com.
3. Lorenzo Pecchi and Gustavo Piga, *Revisiting Keynes*, (MIT, 2008), p.92.

4. Geoff Crocker, *Basic Income and Sovereign Money*, (Palgrave, 2020).
5. https://www.bath.ac.uk/publications/technological-change-and-growth-regimes/attachments/Technological_growth_regimes_FINAL.pdf.
6. Loukas Karabarbounis and Brent Neiman, 'Declining Labour Share', *National Bureau of Economic Research (NBER)*, (2013).
7. Cambridge Econometrics, 'The Macroeconomics of Basic Income', 2022. https://www.camecon.com/what/our-work/the-macroeconomics-of-basic-income/.
8. Joe Chrisp et al. *UBI-eh*? (IPR Bath, 2023) https://www.bath.ac.uk/publications/ubi-eh/.
9. John Maynard Keynes, 'Radio Interview', 1942.
10. Rachel Reeves, 'Chancellor Statement on Public Spending Inheritance', 2024, https://www.gov.uk/government/speeches/chancellor-statement-on-public-spending-inheritance.

On Income

Abstract This chapter examines the relationship between automation, income, and inequality. I postulate that increasing automation reduces waged income, necessitating an increase in social welfare. I then explore the structural causes of income inadequacy, highlighting how technological advancements decrease labour demand and exacerbate wage inequality. Using UK data, I illustrate the growing disparity between high-income professionals and low-wage workers, showing the failure of work and current welfare policies to mitigate poverty. I propose a hybrid income system combining a low universal basic income with increased targeted welfare with reduced conditionality, to address these challenges.

Keywords Automation · Wage inequality · Labour share · Social welfare · Universal basic income (UBI) · Targeted welfare · Conditionality · UK income data · Poverty · Hybrid income system

> POSTULATE: For any given level of GDP, further automation will reduce waged income and require an increase in social welfare income.

It's difficult to hold all other things equal (*'ceteris paribus'*) to test this claim in isolation. The claim also runs into political resistance, since work and wage are assumed as the fundamental source of income, and governments want to constrain social spending. Nevertheless, the phenomena of inadequate income and income inequality are well documented, and require convincing explanation and an effective policy response. If technology does inevitably decrease waged income, and equally inevitably requires increased welfare income, then economic policy will have to accept these inevitabilities, and adapt to address them. That requires a shift in social and political philosophy to accept that high wage work cannot be the source of adequate income for the whole population.

The objective of the economy is to deliver at least an adequate supply of goods and services to everyone. We'll consider the production of these goods and services more in the section of this book below dealing with technology. But in order for people to be able to access the goods and services which the production side of the economy makes available, consumers need to have adequate income to purchase them at the prices at which they can be produced. So the economy needs to deliver adequate consumer income to everyone, often measured as household income.

In the real economy, and therefore in any relevant model of the economy, consumer income derives from 5 main sources, i.e., wages, pensions, dividends, welfare benefits, and household debt or de-saving. The focus on income interacts with the focus on technology, in that automation of production of goods and services inevitably reduces the labour and wage content per unit of output, creating a reduction in the labour share of the aggregate economy. This in turn creates income inadequacy for households and individuals. In an ultimate case, if the production of all goods and services were totally automated, without any employed labour, then all individual and household income would have to be non-labour income. Technology therefore argues for a proportionate increase in non-labour, or social welfare income.

A Profile of UK Household Income

Poverty is a definition of inadequate income. The Joseph Rowntree Foundation's 2024 report[1] on UK poverty, shows that 14.4 million people i.e. 22% of the UK population are in poverty. Of these, 6 million are in deep poverty compared to 4.5 million in 2000, and 4 million are in destitution, a growth of 148% from 5 years previously, all of which the report calls 'social failure at scale' (p. 4).

Neither work nor welfare benefits are sufficient to mitigate this poverty. 15% of working age adults living in a household with someone in work, are in poverty (p. 77). The basic rate of Universal Credit is below the destitution income level (p. 12). 49% of Universal Credit recipients are in poverty (p. 87). Housing costs are a significant factor causing poverty. The 2 child limit on welfare benefits and the benefit cap mean that benefits are too low, particularly for larger families with children, and for lone parent families. Food insecurity, poor health, and low education outcomes are characteristic of families in poverty. Child poverty is greater than pensioner poverty. The JRF 2023 report showed that within the poorest 20% of the population, 50% are in arrears, 25% take out credit to pay essential bills, and 70% go without essentials. A 2021 IPPR report[2] also identifies extensive in-work poverty, meaning that work does not provide adequate income for all members of society.

The UK Office of National Statistics provides an extensive analysis of UK household income. Its most recent report covers the period 1977–2022.[3] Highlights from the report are—

Figure 1: Over a period of nearly 50 years, real mean household income grew by a factor of 2.5. Within this, retired people's real mean income grew by a factor of 3.

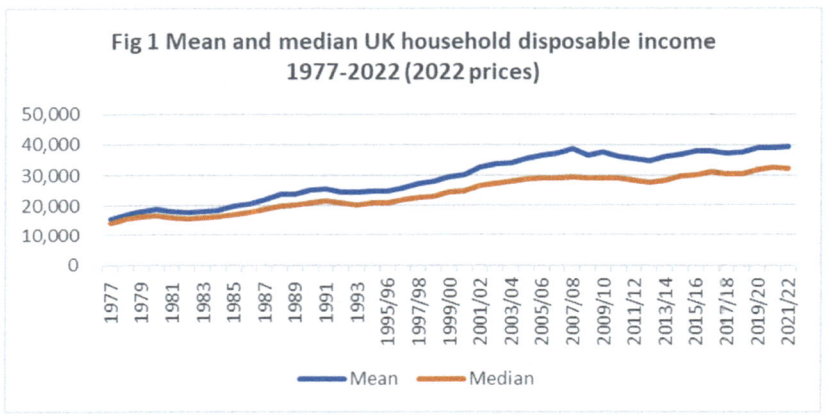

Source ONS Households Disposable Income and Expenditure dataset: www.ons.gov.uk/peoplepopulationandcommunity/personalandhouseholdfinances/incomeandwealth/datasets/householddisposableincomeandinequality Table 1: Timeseries of mean and median equivalised household disposable income, 1977–2021/22, UK [2021/22 prices]

Figure 2: Within this apparently very substantial total growth in real incomes, distributional analysis shows a very different picture for low income groups of the population. The incomes of the highest income households grew by a factor of 2.6, whilst those of the lowest income households grew by a factor of only 1.8, representing a substantial increase in inequality. It was only after the year 2000 that the incomes of the lowest income households began to grow at all.

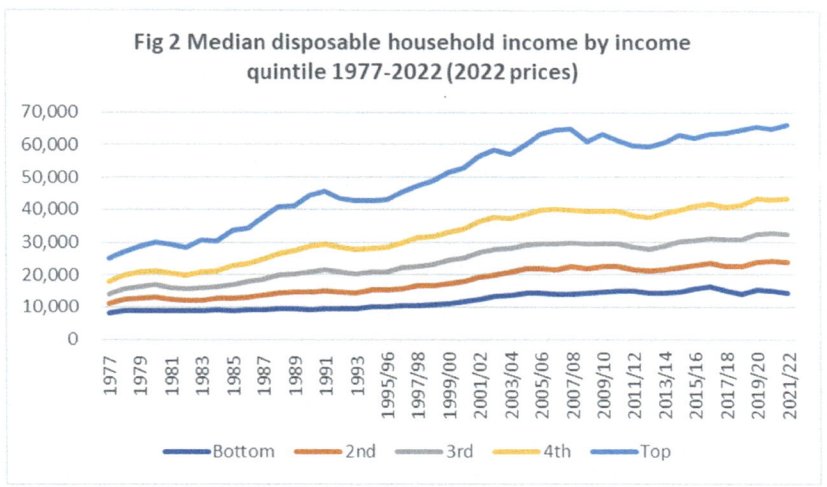

Source ONS Households Disposable Income and Expenditure dataset: www.ons.gov.uk/peoplepopulationandcommunity/personalandhouseholdfinances/incomeandwealth/datasets/householddisposableincomeandinequality Table 2: Timeseries of median equivalised disposable household income of individuals by income quintile, 1977–2021/22, UK [2021/22 prices]

Figure 3 shows current income inequality. In 2022, the highest income fifth of households received 43% of total household income, whilst the bottom income fifth of households received a share of only 7%. Corresponding inequality in the US is even worse, with the lowest income fifth of households receiving only a 3.1% share, the second quintile a 8.3% share and the top income quintile a 51.9% share.

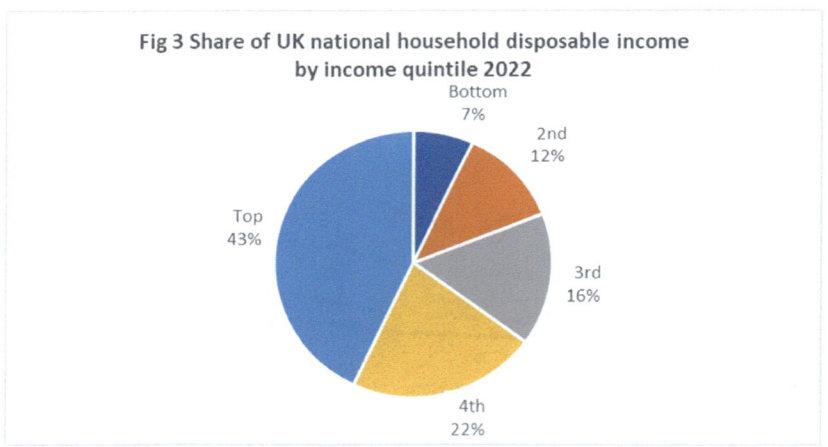

Source ONS Households Disposable Income and Expenditure dataset: www.ons.gov.uk/peoplepopulationandcommunity/personalandhouseholdfinances/incomeandwealth/datasets/householddisposableincomeandinequality Table 4: Percentage shares of equivalised household income and Gini coefficients, ALL individuals, RETIRED individuals and NON-RETIRED individuals, 2021/22, UK

Figure 4: The picture of inequality worsens for working families with children. The incomes of the highest income households grew by a factor of 3, whilst those of the lowest income households grew by only 1.6, i.e. by roughly half as much.

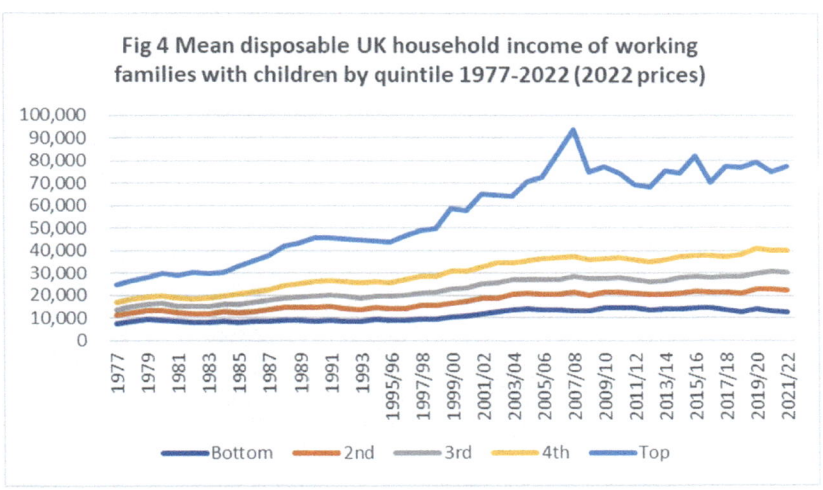

Source ONS Households Disposable Income and Expenditure dataset: www.ons.gov.uk/peoplepopulationandcommunity/personalandhouseholdfinances/incomeandwealth/datasets/householddisposableincomeandinequality Table 5: Mean equivalised disposable household income by quintile for all individuals in non-retired households with children, 1977–2021/22, UK [2021/22 prices]

Figure 5: Whilst wage is 89% of income for all individuals, it is only 53% of income for the lowest income individuals, who therefore rely on benefits for 47% of their income.

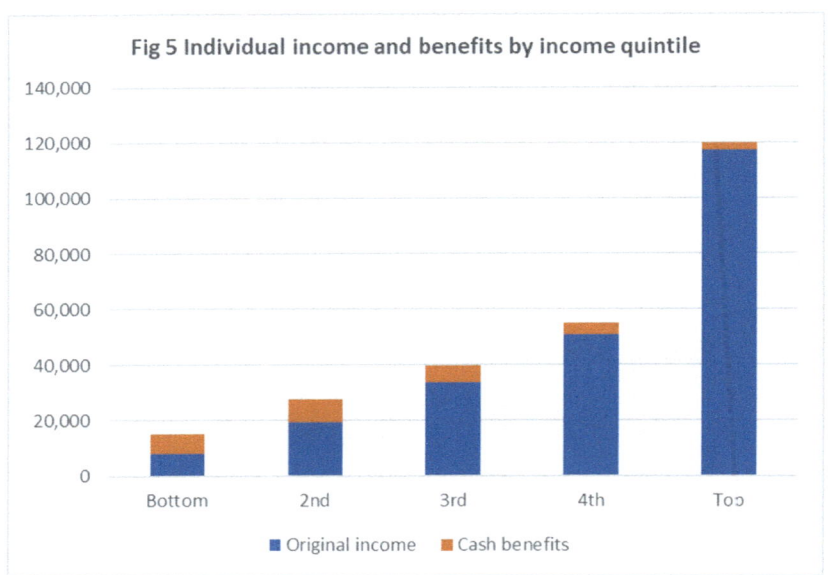

Source ONS Households Disposable Income and Expenditure dataset: www.ons.gov.uk/peoplepopulationandcommunity/personalandhouseholdfinances/incomeandwealth/datasets/householddisposableincomeandinequality Table 12: Summary of the effects of taxes and benefits on ALL individuals by quintile group, 2021/22, UK

Figure 6: Tax and NIC is progressive but only reduces the multiple of highest incomes to lowest incomes from 7.8 to 6.3.

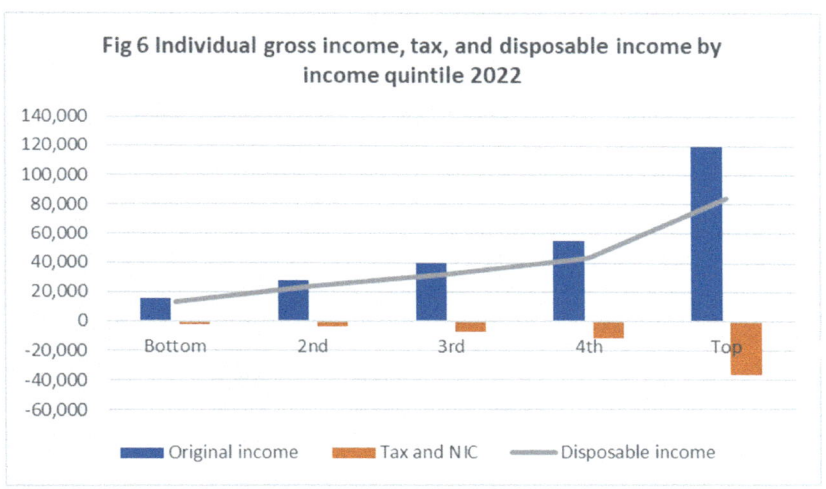

Source ONS Households Disposable Income and Expenditure dataset: www.ons.gov.uk/peoplepopulationandcommunity/personalandhouseholdfinances/incomeandwealth/datasets/householddisposableincomeandinequality Table 12: Summary of the effects of taxes and benefits on ALL individuals by quintile group, 2021/22, UK

Figure 7: Investments and pensions also contribute to income. It is notable that the highest income households earn more from investments (£9672), than lowest income households earn from wages and salaries (£7567).

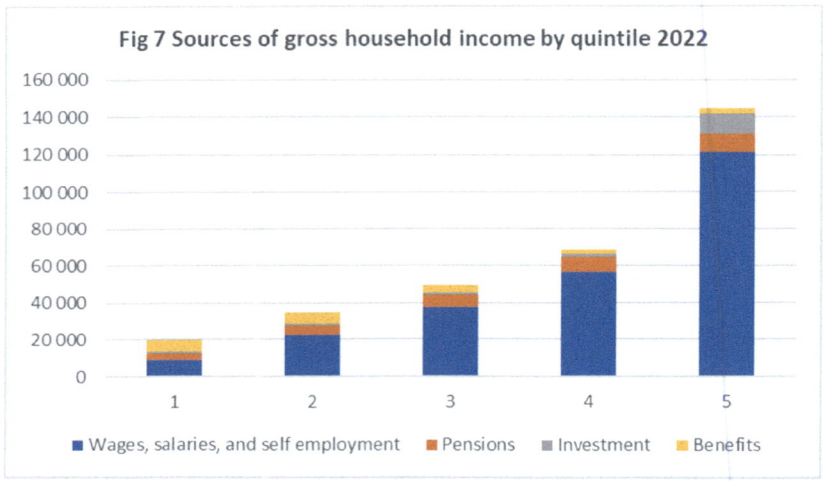

Source ONS Households Disposable Income and Expenditure dataset: www.ons.gov.uk/peoplepopulationandcommunity/personalandhouseholdfinances/incomeandwealth/datasets/householddisposableincomeandinequality Table 13: Average household incomes, taxes and benefits of ALL individuals by quintile group, 2021/22, UK

Figure 8: Whilst the lowest income households pay only 3% of the income tax paid by the highest income households, they pay a much larger amount in Council tax net of rebates, equal to 60% of the Council tax paid by the highest income households. Council tax is hugely regressive.

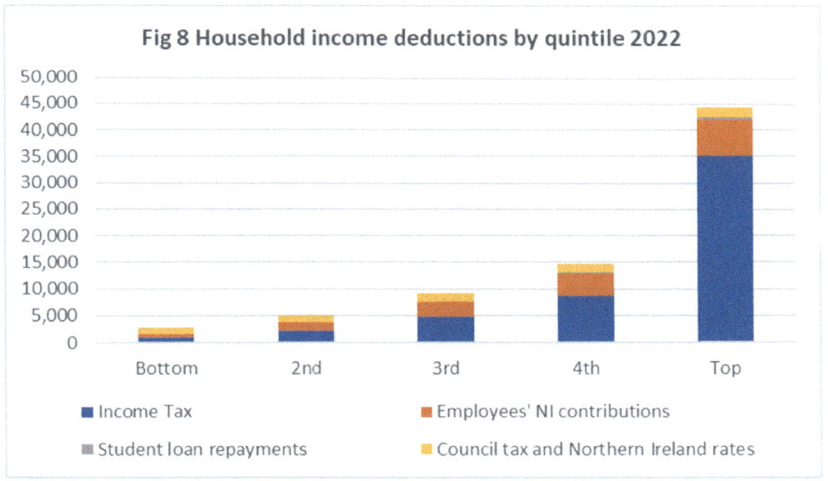

Source ONS Households Disposable Income and Expenditure dataset: www.ons.gov.uk/peoplepopulationandcommunity/personalandhouseholdfinances/incomeandwealth/datasets/householddisposableincomeandinequality Table 13: Average household incomes, taxes and benefits of ALL individuals by quintile group, 2021/22, UK

Figure 9: Over nearly 50 years, the source of household income has shifted slightly. Pensions have increased from 2 to 6% of household income and dividends from 2 to 5%. Benefits swing between 11 and 16% of household income, whilst wages, salaries, and self-employed income reduced from 80 to 74% with a small recent recovery to 78%. This shows that wages and benefits are the most vulnerable sources of income and therefore those of most concern.

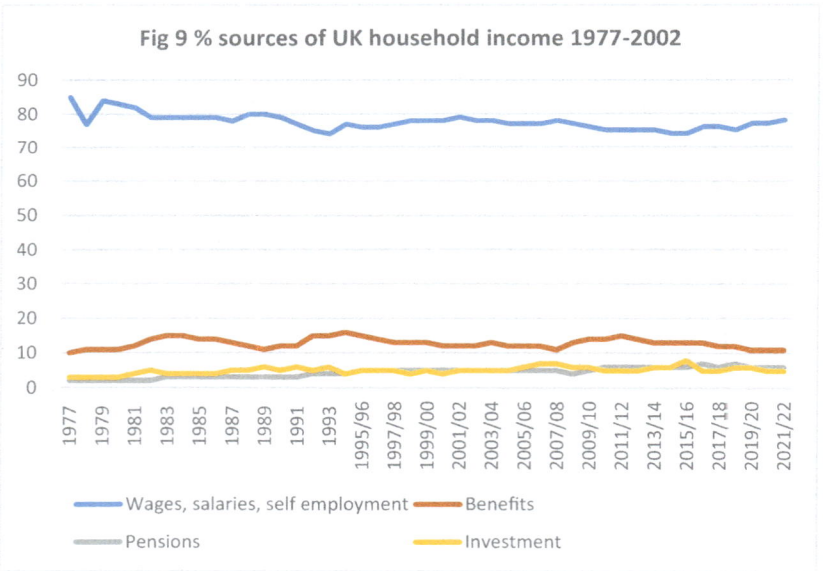

Source ONS Households Disposable Income and Expenditure dataset: www.ons.gov.uk/peoplepopulationandcommunity/personalandhouseholdfinances/incomeandwealth/datasets/householddisposableincomeandinequality Table 28: Income and source of income for all UK households, 1977 to 2021/22 [2021/22 prices]

Relating Household Debt to Income

Figure 10: Essential expenditure in excess of income means that 36% of lowest income households have financial debt, whilst only 13% have a house mortgage.

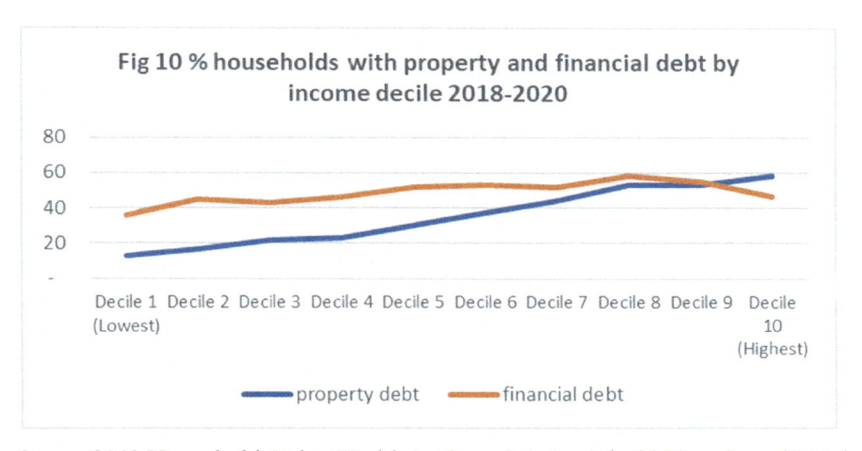

Fig 10 % households with property and financial debt by income decile 2018-2020

[Chart showing property debt and financial debt across Decile 1 (Lowest) through Decile 10 (Highest)]

Source ONS Household Debt: Wealth in Great Britain, July 2010 to June 2016/ April 2014 to March 2020 www.ons.gov.uk/peoplepopulationandcommunity/ personalandhouseholdfinances/incomeandwealth/datasets/householddebtwealt hingreatbritain Table 7.4 Percentage of households with household debt and summary statistics by components, by total household net equivalised income decile1,2,3

The concern is then that low income households resort to debt to supplement inadequate earnings. Household debt can correlate with income in two opposite ways. On the one hand, higher income is required to qualify for loans, so that income and debt are positively correlated, and the borrower has adequate future income to meet the loan repayments. On the other hand, low income may force households into debt, as in the case of so-called 'payday' loans sold at very high interest rates, so that the correlation is negative. The following graphs explore possible connectivity between disposable income and household debt.

Figure 11: Net acquisition of loans for all types of loan for the UK economy as a percentage of GDP grew rapidly up to the 2007 financial crisis.

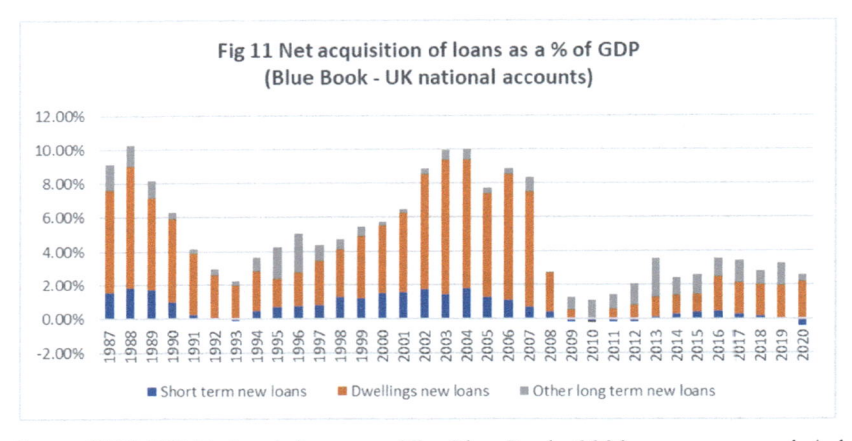

Source ONS UK National Accounts, The Blue Book: 2023 www.ons.gov.uk/releases/uknationalaccountsthebluebook2023

Figure 12: Gross disposable income for the same period shows a clear match whereby new household debt compensates for reductions in gross disposable income.

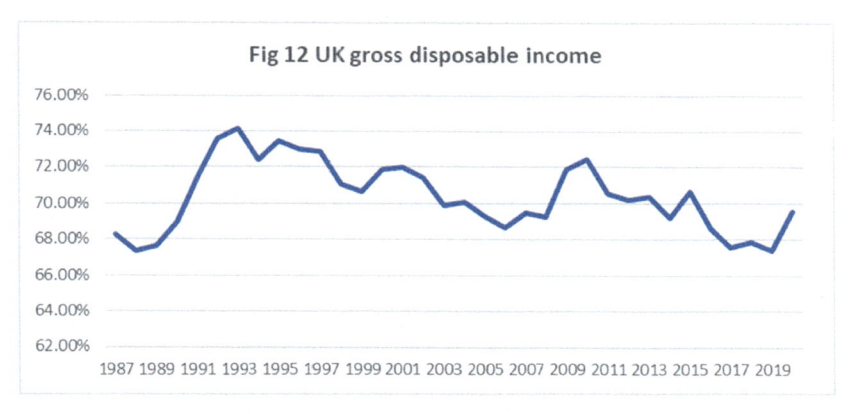

Fig 12 UK gross disposable income

Source ONS Households Disposable Income and Expenditure dataset: www.ons.gov.uk/peoplepopulationandcommunity/personalandhouseholdfinances/incomeandwealth/datasets/householddisposableincomeandinequality Table 1 UK household disposable income 1977–2022 [2022 prices]

The period 1998–2008 saw consumer per capita expenditure exceed income, funded by new household debt.[4]

22   GEOFF CROCKER

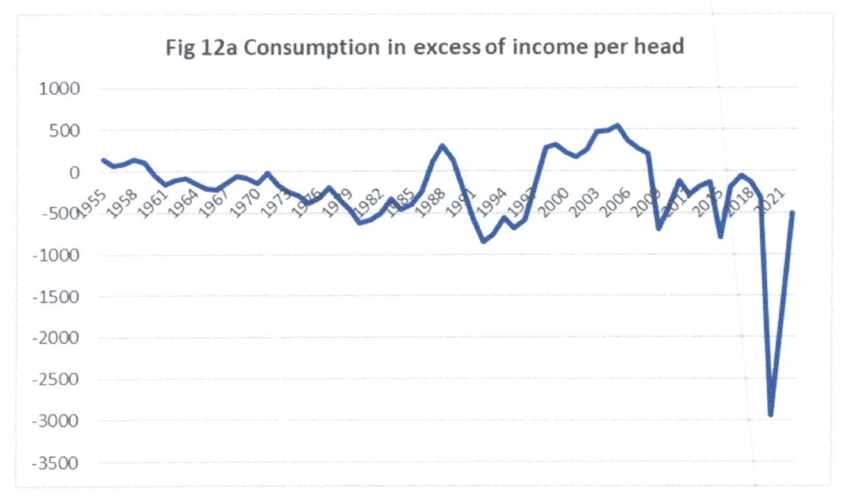

Fig 12a Consumption in excess of income per head

Source ONS Household final consumption expenditure: National concept CVM SA—£m www.ons.gov.uk/economy/nationalaccounts/satelliteaccounts/timeseries/abjr/pn2

The hypothesis that reduced disposable income led to increased household debt can be researched both over time for one country economy, and between economies in one time period.

Figure 13 explores the difference between gross disposable income and consumption expenditure against equity withdrawals in the UK economy, i.e. new borrowing secured against housing assets but used for consumption, against gross disposable income over the 30 year period 1990–2020. This shows a clear correlation which suggests that decreased sufficiency of disposable income for consumption generates increased debt. This phenomenon may be deliberate and manageable for high income households who fund increased consumption by debt repaid from future income, but may be forced on to lower income households who need extra funds for necessary expenditure, and are forced to resort to debt.[5]

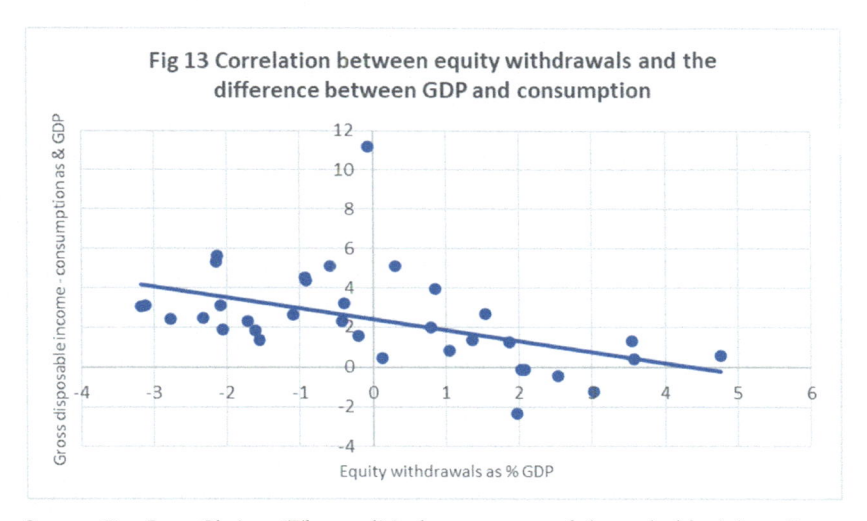

Fig 13 Correlation between equity withdrawals and the difference between GDP and consumption

Source Dr Joe Chrisp 'The political economy of household debt, disposable income and consumption' Institute for Policy Research at the University of Bath, February 2024, Fig. 16 Reproduced with permission www.bath.ac.uk/publications/the-political-economy-of-household-debt-disposable-income-and-consumption

Figure 14: International comparison shows that debt increases with reductions in gross disposable income for the US, UK, and Canadian economies.

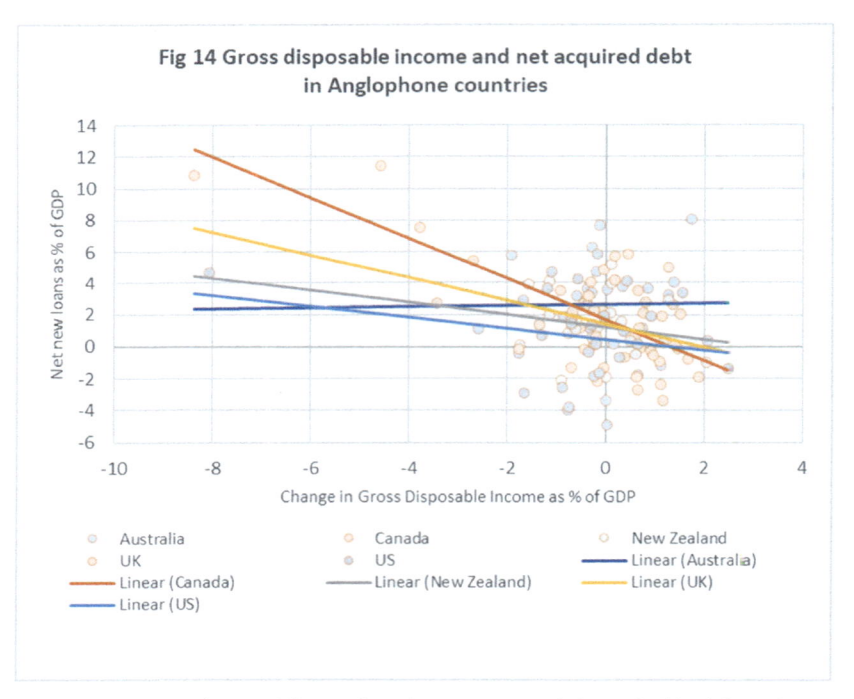

Fig 14 Gross disposable income and net acquired debt in Anglophone countries

Source Dr Joe Chrisp 'The political economy of household debt, disposable income and consumption' Institute for Policy Research at the University of Bath, February 2024, Fig. 25 Reproduced with permission www.bath.ac.uk/publications/the-political-economy-of-household-debt-disposable-income-and-consumption

Household debt has grown massively in most economies, and this has been matched by reductions in the aggregate labour share of GDP.

Figure 15: Household debt in OECD countries grew from 43% of GDP to 68% of GDP over the 25 year period 1995–2020.

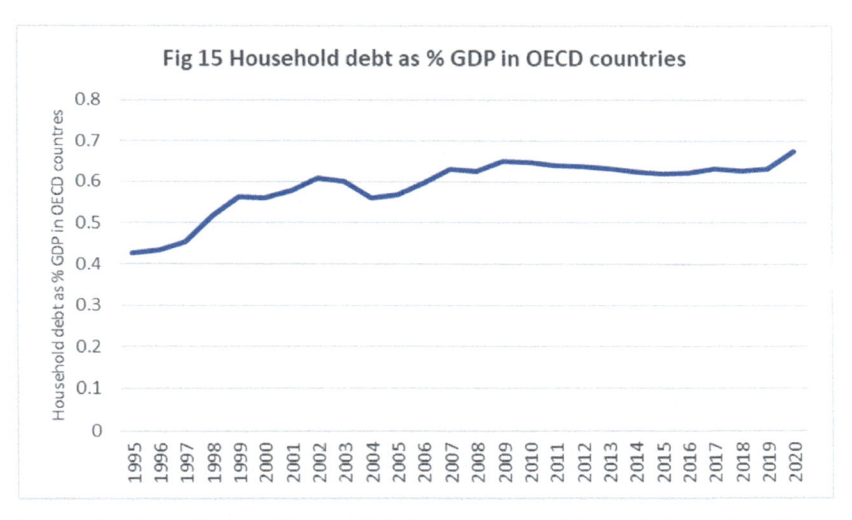

Source Dr Joe Chrisp 'The political economy of household debt, disposable income and consumption' Institute for Policy Research at the University of Bath, February 2024, Fig. 1 Reproduced with permission www.bath.ac.uk/publications/the-political-economy-of-household-debt-disposable-income-and-consumption

26　GEOFF CROCKER

Figure 16: The UK economy experienced an even greater growth of household debt from 57% of GDP to nearly 100% in year 2008.

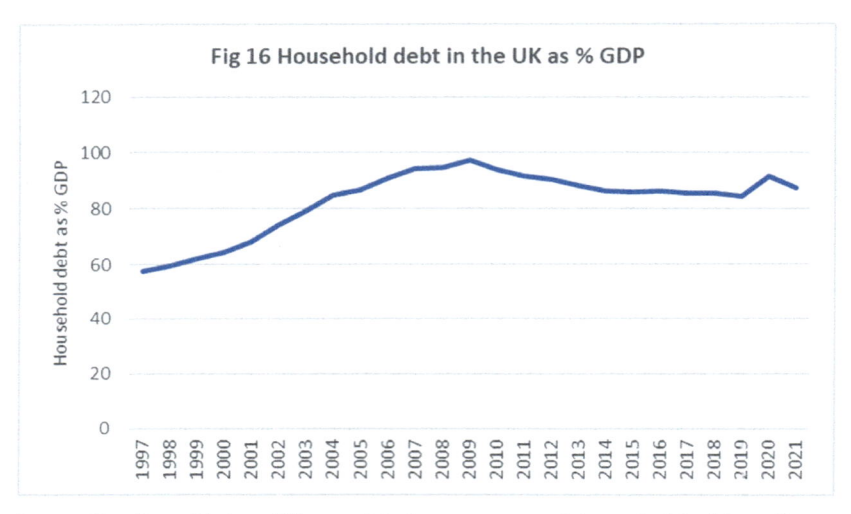

Fig 16 Household debt in the UK as % GDP

Source Dr Joe Chrisp 'The political economy of household debt, disposable income and consumption' Institute for Policy Research at the University of Bath, February 2024, Fig. 2 Reproduced with permission www.bath.ac.uk/publications/the-political-economy-of-household-debt-disposable-income-and-consumption

Figure 17: Similar growth in household debt occurred in other economies, but at a lower rate in France and Sweden, with subsequent reductions in Germany and the US.

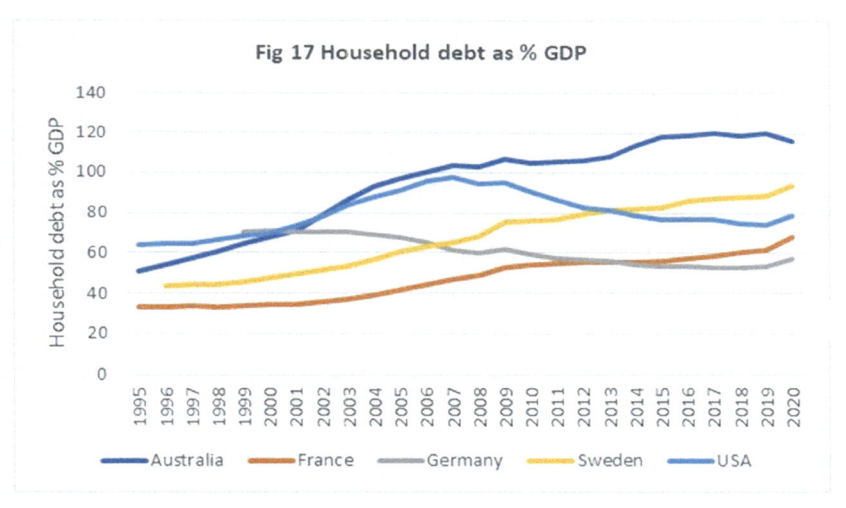

Source Dr Joe Chrisp 'The political economy of household debt, disposable income and consumption' Institute for Policy Research at the University of Bath, February 2024, Fig. 3 Reproduced with permission www.bath.ac.uk/publications/the-political-economy-of-household-debt-disposable-income-and-consumption

Figure 18: It is clear that this increase in household debt occurred in a context of reduced labour share of GDP.

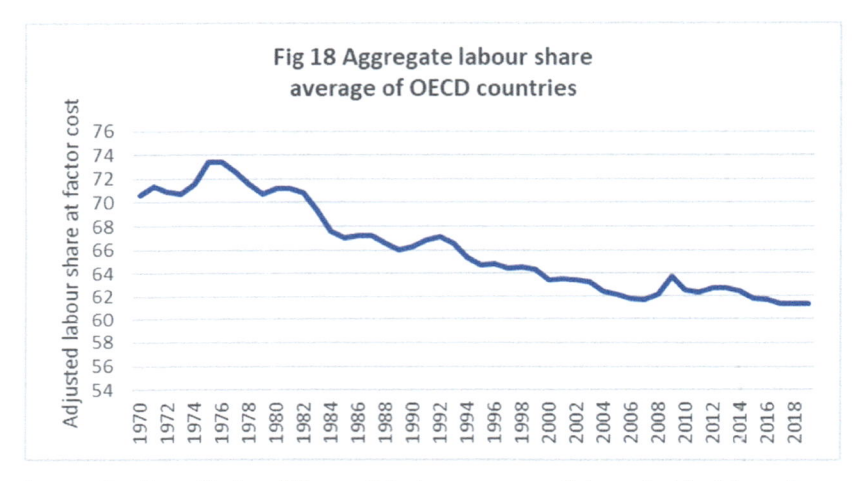

Fig 18 Aggregate labour share average of OECD countries

Source Dr Joe Chrisp 'The political economy of household debt, disposable income and consumption' Institute for Policy Research at the University of Bath, February 2024, Fig. 4 Reproduced with permission www.bath.ac.uk/publications/the-political-economy-of-household-debt-disposable-income-and-consumption

The above analysis offers strong support for the concern that inadequate household income, an inevitable result of the decline in the labour share of GDP, leads to increased household debt. From the limited cases where the data is available by income quintile, it is likely to be particularly true for the low income quintile that unmanageable household debt, initially taken out to compensate for deficient earned income, rapidly becomes unrepayable from the same future constrained income. This is part of the vicious circle of poverty.

The analysis shows the relevance of the claim that the twin urgent need for economic policy is to get adequate income to people, and to get debt out of the economy. The associated twin questions are what causes inadequate income and associated debt, and what are the most effective remedies?

In developing the best explanation for these twin phenomena, a radically different diagnostic of the 2007 economic crisis may emerge, i.e. that the crisis was not caused by the behavioural fault of banks over-lending, and governments under-regulating, but by a structural fault in the economy, failing to provide adequate consumer income against adequate supply, thereby generating debt.

The Structure of Income

As Fig. 9 above shows, currently UK average household income comprises

- 78% wages, salaries and self-employment income
- 11% benefits
- 6% pensions
- 5% dividends

This varies considerably by income group, which ONS reports[6] as (Table 1).

Table 1 Income structure by group

Income group	% income received as			
	Wage, salary, self-employ (%)	Benefits (%)	Pensions (%)	Dividends (%)
Top professional	89	3	3	5
Long term unemployed	32	63	1	2

Pensions and dividends have increased their share of income over the long term, and appear reasonably secure. Waged earnings are extremely unequal, both in their quantity and their security. High income professionals have seen their share of aggregate earnings grow remarkably, and generally have high income security. Low income groups suffer from insecure employment, and the precarity of the gig economy.

Work has long been seen as the prime source of income, economically, politically, and ethically. Even Keynes focussed on work and wage as income, and the source of effective demand, with its multiplier effect when spent in the economy to stimulate investment. He made no recommendation about welfare benefits.[7] He was dismissive of C H Douglas's call for a universal basic income. His call was for full employment, which he saw as the remedy to social deprivation.[8] Full employment has long been the leading economic policy espoused and proclaimed by a wide range of political parties.

Welfare benefits have been considered ethical and necessary for certain groups such as children, the retired, and disabled people. Otherwise welfare policy is typically designed to force people to work, on the assumption that adequately waged work is available. Work is the ethical imperative. The political vision is always for a high-employment high-wage economy.

Moreover, governments expect the workplace to bear social costs, for example for sick pay and pensions, on the questionable assumption that the product price can bear social costs in internationally competitive product markets, and with the intention of avoiding meeting social costs from government social budgets. This is particularly clear in the current insistence on increasing the retirement age. Not only is this a breach of trust to people who have worked long years in the expectation of a retirement pension, but its effects on industrial productivity are unclear, and may well be negative. Retaining people aged over 65 in the workforce might have the effect of increasing output, but this is not at all certain, and in some cases unlikely. The increased retirement age has not resulted in noticeable growth in GDP. It could equally either reduce productivity measured as output/person, and/or reduce job opportunities for young people entering the workforce. Individual productivity, or effectiveness, or innovative inspiration, may well, and at some point definitely does, decline with age. It's a valid hypothesis that the UK's lack of productivity is a result of its increased retirement pension age. However, a recent study (Hernæs, Kornstad, Markussen, Røed, (2023) 'Ageing and labour productivity', Labour Economics[9]) of extended employment beyond the previous retirement age in Norway suggests that firm productivity is only slightly affected, but new employment of younger people may decline. More macroeconomic evidence is needed.

Governments fear that assuming greater social responsibility for what are essentially social costs would drive up the need for further government borrowing, adding to the already unsustainable level of government debt. This is a perspective which will be examined in the section on rethinking money below.

Work is not only the prime source of income. It also provides identity and role, creative interaction, friendship, and personal flourishing. But work is changing, largely through technology, which is why economic theory needs to incorporate technology explicitly and centrally into all its models. Working hours per week have been in consistent decline for decades. Keynes famously predicted a 15 hour working week.[10] So far, productivity gains have been taken as greater output and consumption instead, but the current acceleration of automation for example in AI, may soon prove him correct.

Figure 19: A long term view of the labour share of income in the UK shows that the share declined for 40 years from 72% in 1955 to 54% in 1995, before stabilising at 60% from year 2000.[11]

Fig 19 UK labour share of income

Source ONS Labour share of income: Whole economy SA: percentage: UK www.ons.gov.uk/employmentandlabourmarket/peopleinwork/labourproductivity/timeseries/fzln/ucst

For convenience, we now refer to all labour income, including wages, salaries, and self-employed income as 'wage'. All other non-labour income, including benefits, pensions and dividends are referred to as 'social' income.

Data reported above demonstrates that wage is insufficient to provide adequate household income. This is particularly evident in that

- wage only provides an annual income of £9266 to the lowest income quintile household
- there is clear empirical evidence of in-work poverty
- wage only contributes 32% of the income needs of the long-term unemployed
- the labour share of GDP has fallen from 70 to 60%
- widespread poverty is observed

Various explanations are possible for these observations, including

- children, the elderly, and some disabled people, cannot take employment, and the composition of the population may be shifting to increase these groups
- production technology increasingly requires either
    - less labour and/or
    - highly skilled labour, reducing demand and wage for low-skilled labour
- rentier capitalism shifts value to capital from labour
- reduced unionisation and bargaining power leads to low wage

The political explanations for wage suppression by rentier capitalism and reduced unionisation fail to explain the huge increases in middle to high income quintile wage, many of whom are neither shareholders nor unionised. An explanation from technology is able to explain both an overall reduction in the demand for labour, and a huge increase in wage inequality in favour of high-skilled work, because new technologies require less low-skilled labour.

Inadequate labour income is therefore essentially due to one or more of 3 factors:

- personal, where a person's age, health, or skillset prevents employment
- political, as in the rentier capital explanation above
- structural, where technology and automation displace labour, as explored in the section on technology below

Policies to enable personal availability to earn labour income range from education and training to raising the retirement age. These will have limited effect if a reduction in labour income derives from an inexorable increased deployment of automation technology.

Policy correctives for wage inadequacy include

- wage increase by legislation
- economic growth
- high wage employment creation
- higher skill-set training
- redistribution by benefit and tax increase
- restructuring income and money

Whilst personal development through training to acquire higher skills is always commendable, there are limits to individual capability. For example, whilst I enjoy playing the piano, no amount of training would render me sufficiently skilled to become a concert pianist. There is simply no market demand for my skill level!

Wage increase by legislation has been enacted by the Minimum Wage. This has been a spectacularly successful policy.

34 GEOFF CROCKER

Figure 20: In the UK, after its introduction in 1999, the Minimum Wage increased in real terms by 38% by 2017, a substantially higher increase than in all other OECD countries except New Zealand.[12]

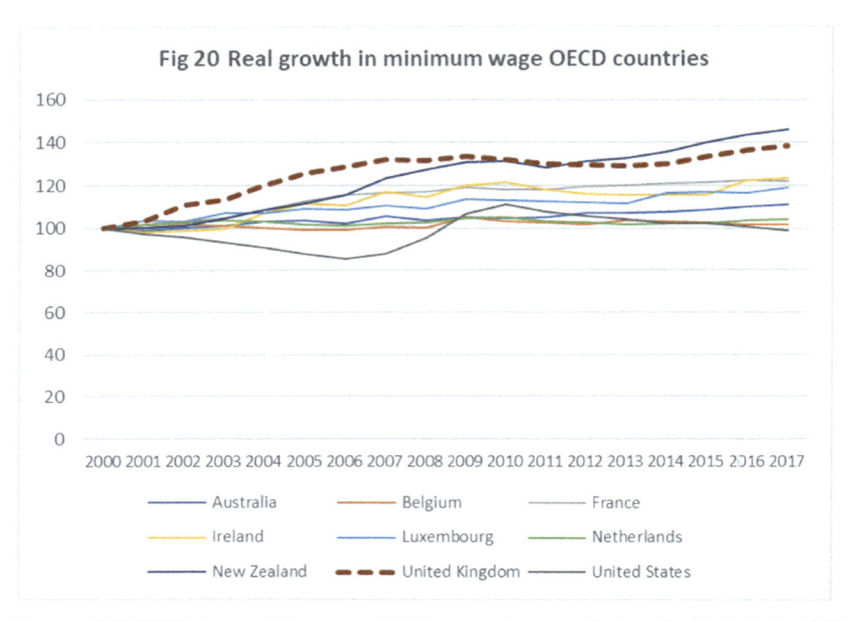

Fig 20 Real growth in minimum wage OECD countries

Series: Australia, Belgium, France, Ireland, Luxembourg, Netherlands, New Zealand, United Kingdom, United States

Source GOV.UK https://assets.publishing.service.gov.uk/media/5c9e3e4e40f0b625e1cbd852/20_years_of_the_National_Minimum_Wage_-_data.xlsx Slide 11 [2]: Change in real minimum wages in OECD countries

Figure 21: As a result of Minimum Wage legislation, the percentage of low paid hourly jobs fell from 22% in 1997 to 8.9% by 2022.[13]

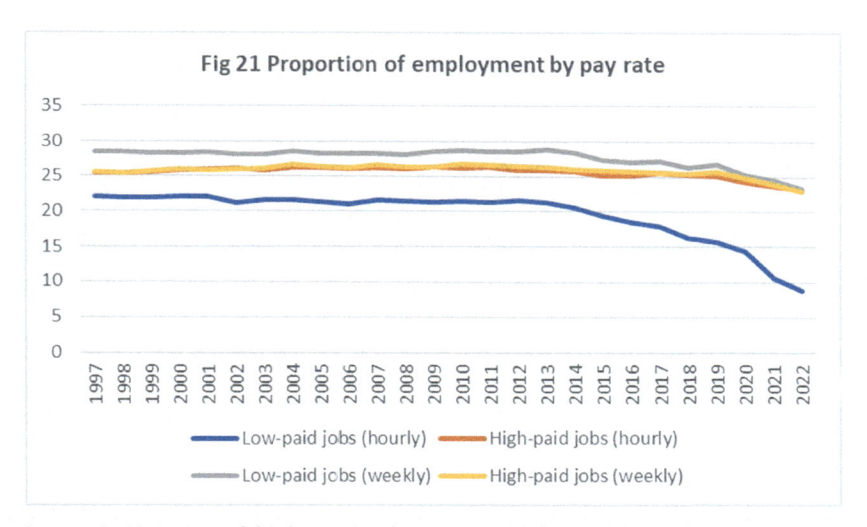

Fig 21 Proportion of employment by pay rate

— Low-paid jobs (hourly) — High-paid jobs (hourly)
— Low-paid jobs (weekly) — High-paid jobs (weekly)

Source ONS Low and high pay in the UK: 2023 https://www.ons.gov.uk/employmentandlabourmarket/peopleinwork/earningsandworkinghours/bulletins/lowandhighpayuk/2023 Fig. 1

Figure 22: Meanwhile, income from welfare benefits has declined over the last 12 years. Expanding the data of Fig. 9 above shows a repeated trend to drive benefits down from 16 to 11% of household income.[14]

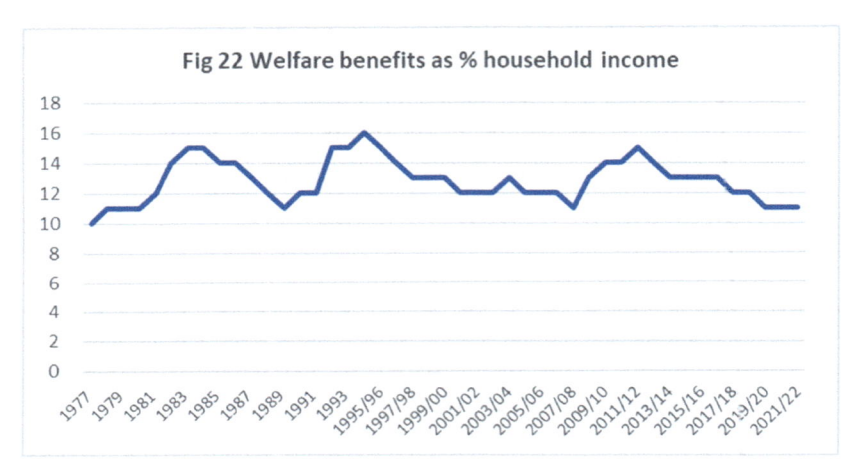

Fig 22 Welfare benefits as % household income

Source ONS Households Disposable Income and Expenditure dataset: www.ons.gov.uk/peoplepopulationandcommunity/personalandhouseholdfinances/incomeandwealth/datasets/householddisposableincomeandinequality Table 28: Income and source of income for all UK households, 1977 to 2021/22 [2021/22 prices]

Figures 23 and 24: Focussing on wage and benefits in the years since the financial crisis, we see that from 2007 to 2012, average household real wage declined by 17% and average household real benefits by 11%. However, from 2012 to 2022, average household real wage recovered to be 1.7% below its 2007 level, whilst average household real benefits declined further to fall by 18.2% from its 2007 level. Whilst average household real total income by 2022 had, but only just, recovered its 2007 level, this masks a major development where, as benefits declined further, household incomes which are more dependent on benefits than on wage, suffered a considerable continuous loss in real household income for the whole 2007–2022 period.

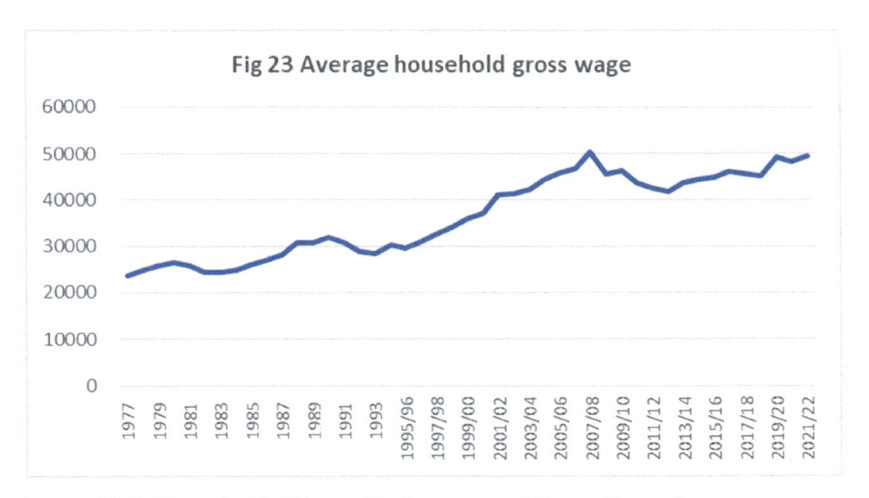

Fig 23 Average household gross wage

Source ONS Households Disposable Income and Expenditure dataset: www.ons.gov.uk/peoplepopulationandcommunity/personalandhouseholdfinances/incomeandwealth/datasets/householddisposableincomeandinequality Table 28: Income and source of income for all UK households, 1977 to 2021/22 [2021/22 prices]

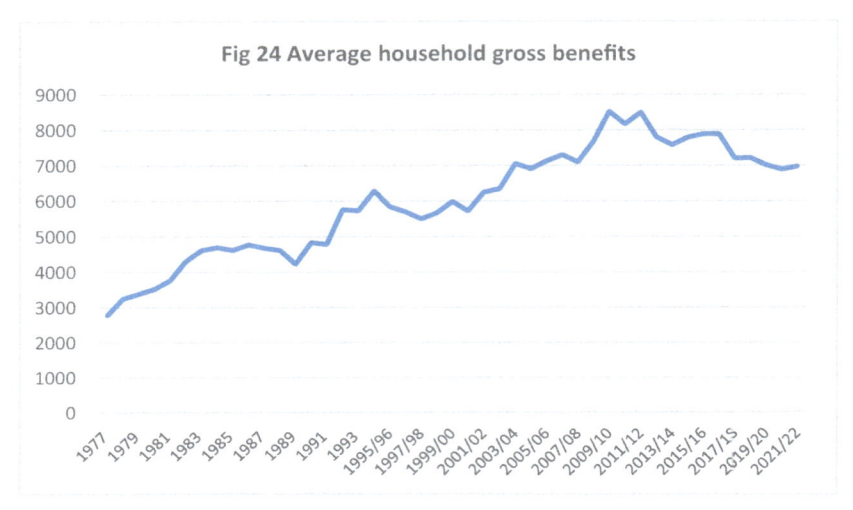

Fig 24 Average household gross benefits

Source ONS Households Disposable Income and Expenditure dataset: www.ons.gov.uk/peoplepopulationandcommunity/personalandhouseholdfinances/incomeandwealth/datasets/householddisposableincomeandinequality Table 28: Income and source of income for all UK households, 1977 to 2021/22 [2021/22 prices]

So, whilst legislative action via the Minimum Wage has had some effect in correcting income inadequacy for low income households, redistribution by benefits has not, but in fact, welfare benefits have been massively reduced, thus greatly reinforcing inequality and poverty. As the Joseph Rowntree report on UK poverty 2023 states, 'the basic rates of benefits are inadequate'.[15]

There is therefore a demonstrable need to increase social income to the income quintiles of the population for whom high wage employment fails to offer adequate income.

The question then is what the level of additional income benefits should be, and whether they should be targeted or universal. Targeted benefits appear to be the more effective option when low income households are identified as needing increased income. Each household would receive more income from an aggregate budget than if the same budget were shared equally, universally. Targeted and therefore necessarily conditional benefits have therefore been the dominant form of welfare in most countries.

However, conditionality imposes some significant negative outcomes, specifically

- the humiliation and intrusion of means testing, and other conditionality enquiries
- consequent low take up rates, especially amongst elderly people
- unemployment and poverty traps as benefit recipients lose benefit as they gain wage
- high administrative system cost

At the same time there are cogent arguments for universality, namely

- everyone has equal entitlement to the benefits of inherited infrastructure and technology
- ecological benefit derives from sourcing income other than from more work and production
- technology allows less work centric lifestyle choices, and therefore human flourishing
- high take up rates
- low administrative system cost
- universality is socially cohesive

The questions are

- whether a universal basic income is feasible in the macroeconomy
- whether the conditionalities of targeted welfare benefits can be moderated to mitigate their defects

Research on these two questions has recently been reported.

Cambridge Econometrics UK used their well-established, dynamically recalibrated macroeconomic model of the UK economy to test the impact of a universal income paid to all adults and funded by direct money financing.[16] The results are that £100bn of universal income, equivalent to some £2000 per person per year, funded by direct money financing, proved to be non-inflationary, as spare capacity in the supply side of the economy met the increased demand generated by the new universal income. Moreover the research showed that, if a further 15% of jobs were lost due to automation, then an amount of universal income equal to the aggregate labour income lost, would incentivise new investment, and hence also produce a non-inflationary outcome.

The Institute for Policy Research at the University of Bath, UK used microeconomic simulation modelling to test the budgetary impact of relaxing conditionality in the current UK welfare system.[17] Their results showed (Table 2).

Table 2 Cumulative gross cost of lower conditionality of targeted welfare benefits

Individual policy reform	*Estimated cumulative gross cost*
Finish migration to Universal Credit (UC)	£1.272bn
Remove wealth and savings from UC means test	£1.897bn
Reduce UC taper rate to 40%	£14.403bn
Increase standard allowance to £120/220/week	£33.863bn
Remove high income child benefit charge	£37.383bn
Scrap 2 child UC limit	£39.56bn
Increase child benefit to £30/week	£46.124bn

These reforms represent a socially improved welfare system. The 40% taper proposed, whereby any welfare recipient would lose only 40% of their welfare benefit when taking paid work, hugely reduces the unemployment trap and the poverty trap of the current Universal Credit system with a taper rate in excess of 70%. Increased benefit rates directly address the income inadequacy and poverty set out above.

A credible proposal is therefore for a hybrid system with a small universal element, together with a reformed targeted component with substantially reduced conditionality.

The distinction between the two elements researched above is in their funding. The Cambridge Econometrics research modelled funding by direct money financing, or the creation of debt-free sovereign money, whilst the IPR Bath reformed targeted benefit scheme is calculated to require an increase of 4.4% in basic tax and 8.8% in higher rate tax if it is to be tax funded.

The question of alternative funding mechanisms leads to the next section on the nature of money.

REFERENCES

1. Joseph Rowntree Foundation, 'UK Poverty 2024: The Essential Guide to Understanding Poverty in the UK', 2024.
2. Institute for Public Policy Research, 'No Longer Managing: The Rise of Working Poverty and Fixing Britain's Social Settlement', 2021, www.ippr.org/research/publications/no-longer-managing.
3. ONS, 'Household Disposable Income and Inequality Dataset', www.ons.gov.uk/peoplepopulationandcommunity/personalandhouseholdfinances/incomeandwealth/datasets/householddisposableincomeandinequality.
4. ONS, 'National Accounts Satellite Accounts: Timeseries', www.ons.gov.uk/economy/nationalaccounts/satelliteaccounts/timeseries/abjr/pn2.
5. Joe Chrisp, '*The Political Economy of Household Debt, Disposable Income, and Consumption*', 2024. www.bath.ac.uk/publications/the-political-economy-of-household-debt-disposable-income-and-consumption/attachments/political-economy-household-debt-disposable-income-consumption.pdf
6. ONS, '*Household Disposable Income and Inequality Dataset*'.
7. John Maynard Keynes, *The General Theory of Employment, Interest, and Money* (London: MacMillan, 1936).
8. Donald Markwell, *John Maynard Keynes and International Relations: Economic Paths to War and Peace* (Oxford: Oxford University Press, 2006).
9. E. Hernæs et al., 'Ageing and Labour Productivity', *Labour Economics*, 2023.
10. John Maynard Keynes, 'Economic Possibilities for Our Grandchildren', in *The Nation and Athenaeum*, 1930.
11. ONS, 'Labour Productivity Timeseries', www.ons.gov.uk/employmentandlabourmarket/peopleinwork/labourproductivity/timeseries/fzln/ucst.
12. UK Government, '20 Years of the National Minimum Wage—Data', 2019.
13. ONS, 'Low and High Pay in the UK', 2023, www.ons.gov.uk/employmentandlabourmarket/peopleinwork/earningsandworkinghours/bulletins/lowandhighpayuk/2023.
14. ONS, 'Household Disposable Income and Inequality Dataset'.

15. Joseph Rowntree Foundation, 'UK Poverty 2024: The Essential Guide to Understanding Poverty in the UK'.
16. Cambridge Econometrics, 'The Macroeconomics of Basic Income', www.camecon.com/what/our-work/the-macroeconomics-of-basic-income/.
17. Institute for Policy Research, 'Steps from UC to UBI'.

On Money

Abstract This chapter investigates the nature of money and its creation, challenging traditional views that treat money as debt. Money is a social construct, created without pre-existing debt. I critique the current reliance on interest rates and debt to manage the economy. I also argue that Quantitative Easing (QE) has been dysfunctional. To reform monetary policy, I propose direct money financing of government expenditure as a more effective and sustainable alternative, highlighting its potential to reduce public debt and avoid austerity, while maintaining economic stability without inflation.

Keywords Money creation · Debt · Quantitative Easing (QE) · Direct money financing · Interest rate · Public debt · Austerity · Monetary policy reform · Inflation

> POSTULATE: Since money does not pre-exist in nature, at the point of its creation, it is not debt
> POSTULATE: When a central bank buys its own government's debt, the result is zero net debt, and equivalent to direct money financing of government expenditure

Way back in 1970, in a student economics tutorial group, the tutor, the late Dr Julian Bharier, held his head in his hands and lamented 'O dear, no-one understands money!'. Over 50 years later, his lament remains valid.

Towards a fuller understanding of money, this section considers

- The 'ontology', or nature of money
- Monetary policy through
    o Interest rate management of the economy
    o Debt funding of private and public sector expenditure
    o Quantitative Easing
        – The dysfunctionality of QE
        – Implications of QE for the redesign of monetary policy
- Proposals for reform of monetary policy
- The superiority of direct money financing of government expenditure.

The 'Ontology' or Nature of Money

We need to consider money from first principles, not from current practice and definitions. Money is **an artefact**, a human construct. It is not a real resource. The historic practice of 'The Gold Standard' attempted to make money a quasi-real resource by linking its creation to the amount of gold held in government vaults. Being convertible to gold was thought to give sufficient confidence to money to persuade people to hold and use money. But it was clearly a totally artificial construct, and no logic existed for restricting the amount of money in circulation to the amount of a mineral dug from the earth. Moreover, when production, consumption, and trading activities of the economy required more money to be in circulation, then the Gold Standard artificially suppressed the amount of money available, and therefore constrained economic activity. The artefact was thus controlling its creator, the tail was truly wagging the dog. Sense prevailed and the Gold Standard was abandoned.

Confidence in an artefact is also **a social construct**. People trust money because people trust money. As long as other people accept money as payment for goods and services, and as payment for their work as wages and salaries, then money is secure. Some schools of thought claim that money derives inherent value due to governments accepting it to pay due taxes. It's a view which might have some validity historically. But today people would lose confidence in money more quickly if it were no longer accepted to buy goods and services, than if it were no longer accepted to pay tax.

The focus on money in economic policy has become as obsessive and misguided as the obsession in mainstream economic theory on price, examined in the chapter on theory below. Households and businesses make sales and purchases from limited money budgets. When a household or business takes a loan, it is truly debt and has a repayment schedule. This is however **a category error** when applied to the aggregate economy, to government expenditure and accounts, and to central bank creation of money.

All money is initially created. It does not pre-exist in nature. Thus, at the point of its creation, it is not pre-owned, not borrowed from any other source, and is therefore not debt. Michael Kumhof et al. in their 2020 paper 'Central Bank Money: Liability, Asset or Equity of the Nation?'[1] make the powerful point that, since a central bank can only repay central bank money with the same central bank money, and is therefore not defaultable, then this money is not a liability of the central bank, and therefore not debt, but should rather be defined as 'social equity'.

Traditionally, money has existed in physical form, whether in metal coins, or paper notes. When created, it has a value, known as its 'face value'. In its physical forms, it also has a physical cost of production. The difference between its face value and its cost of production is defined as **'seigniorage'**. The value of this seigniorage accrues to the agency which is allowed to create this money. It has occasionally but rarely been the case that coinage has had negative seigniorage. Seventeenth-century British coins had a higher metal value than their face value and were therefore illegally exported to France and melted down for their value as bullion. Money, therefore, at its point of creation, has a face value, a production cost, and a net seigniorage. It does not have any associated debt. Currently, most money is created and exists as digital money. The marginal cost of producing digital money is close to zero, so that seigniorage is now almost equal to the full face value of digital money. In addition to this seigniorage from money creation, seigniorage also arises through the interest rate on money being often much lower than the return on the assets backing the money.

Money is created by commercial banks when they make loans to individuals and businesses. But curiously, in most jurisdictions, including the US, EU, UK, and Japan, governments and their central banks are not allowed to create money to fund government expenditure, a practice known as direct money financing. The prohibition is intended to prevent government profligacy, a curious claim of irresponsibility when the same government is trusted with the nuclear button, and other significant responsibilities. Instead, governments are forced to borrow money to fund their expenditure. In effect, government is borrowing money it has allowed commercial banks to create!

Governments and commentators often say that there is no 'magic money tree'. In fact there is. Money, as we have seen, can be created digitally at zero marginal cost, at a keystroke from 'thin air'. This does not mean that there are no constraints to money creation. The question is not whether money should be created, but how much should be created. Many people are singularly aware of the economic histories of the Weimar Republic and of Zimbabwe, when excess money creation rendered the currency worthless, with consequent collapse of the economy. But those extreme exceptions required a breakdown in the real supply side of the economy.

We also need to understand that government financial balances are an intermediate variable in the economy, and not an exogenous real constraint. They do not determine 'what we can afford'. As Keynes said, 'anything we can actually do, we can afford'.[2] This principle of real resource economics should guide economic policy, rather than the overextended practice of financial accountancy.

There is a fundamental distinction between the nature of money in economics, and in accountancy. Accountancy assumes the pre-existence of money, and a current limit to the total quantity of money in circulation, whereas economics accepts the creation of money. Accountancy insists on its methodology of double-entry accounting, where all accounts should balance. But where money is created digitally, essentially from nothing, then an imbalance is inevitably introduced into the financial system. In particular, insisting on an accounting balance in central banks' balance sheet is imposing an artifice on the reality of money creation. Discussion and debate are needed on how this paradox is best resolved.

> **Economics vs Accountancy—Competing Paradigms**
>
> Economics is concerned with **real** variables, viz
>
> - the output of goods and services
> - consumption
> - employment
> - investment
> - productivity
> - government expenditure
> - imports and exports
> - resources
>
>   o primarily of land, labour, and time
>   o secondarily of their derivatives of infrastructure, capital equipment, labour skill mix, and technology
>
> - standard of living
> - distribution of income
>
> The only common variable for measuring the real variables of economics is the unit of currency. Hence they become represented as financial variables, and economics becomes apparently equivalent to accountancy. This inevitable use of a shared unit of measure masks key differences which are crucial for economic management and policy debate.
>
> Productivity is a key economic variable which determines prosperity, but which crucially needs to be measured in real terms, i.e. in real units of output per real hour of work. This can be difficult to measure over time, since products change and improve their specification. But reporting productivity in financial values incorporates product price and labour wage, and since real productivity will

have generally reduced real prices, it gets double counted or at least obscured if productivity is measured by value.

Accountancy insists on its methodology of 'double-entry accounting' and 'balance sheets'. Income and expenditure accounts and balance sheets must ultimately be equal to, or exceed, zero. The main constraint is financial balances, i.e. money. The accountancy paradigm is appropriate for microeconomic units of individuals, households, and businesses.

However, its transference to apply to economic aggregates, and the macroeconomy, is a category error. The main distinctives which arise between economics and accountancy paradigms are those of constraints, and therefore of affordability. In accountancy the constraint is financial resource; in economics it is real resource. The essential difference is that government, operating at the macroeconomic level considering real resources, can, does, and must create money. Individuals, households, and businesses cannot.

Double-entry accounting is unable to represent the real process of money creation. Today, most money is created digitally at zero production cost, literally 'out of thin air'. The creating agency enjoys 100% seigniorage, i.e. the difference between the face value of the money and the cost of producing it. An inevitable huge imbalance is created with zero on one side. Double-entry accounting is inadequate to represent this reality; hence the need for redefinition of central banks' 'balance sheets'.

Discussion of money creation frequently leads to pejorative cries of 'printing money' and consequent hyper-inflation. Everyone knows about Weimar and Zimbabwe. This knee-jerk reaction avoids the need to determine the quantity of money which is needed to service the real economy, particularly to finance consumption and investment to create real economic growth. Insufficiency of money to enable growth in the real economy is what led historically to abandonment of the Gold Standard. It may equally lead to a contemporary need to abandon so-called fiscal rules.

If we imagine extremes, in a situation surrounded by ample real resources but with no money issued, an accountant would conclude that we couldn't afford anything, whilst an economist would predict an affluent lifestyle. Or if real resources were scant but money abundant, then accountancy would determine immediate affordability, but the economist would predict poverty and inflation.

The key question is whether financial measures correctly report real measures. Specifically, does a government budget of tax revenues and government expenditure, whether in deficit or surplus, balanced by borrowing as debt or its repayment, match real resource availability, and constraint? The standard fear is that if consumer and government expenditure measured financially exceeds supply, then rampant inflation will ensue. But this is not necessarily so, if a position is possible where real resources remain available, even when money in financial accounting, is not.

Keynesian macroeconomic models of the economy rarely lead to price inflation, but rather expect increased demand to firstly engage any excess capacity in the real economy, measured for example by industrial capacity utilisation, and then to stimulate investment to increase real supply. This follows Keynes's dismissal of 'Say's Law' that supply creates its own demand, replacing it with 'Keynes's Law' that, on the contrary, demand creates its own supply. The supply side of the economy can respond to demand with production and investment, but demand cannot respond to a supply increase if it lacks the necessary income, which is why Keynes argued against wage reduction in a recession.

According to accountancy, government financial balances are a binding constraint. According to economics they are not necessarily so. Rather they are an intermediate variable in the economy. So, if it is possible to have real resources available whilst the government's financial budget hits its limit, then we face a real danger of running the economy at less than full employment of real resources. Those real resources include labour. Hence the classic Keynesian worry of involuntary, unnecessary unemployment. Accountancy's definition of affordability is the financial budget. The Keynesian economics definition of affordability is that 'anything we can actually do, we can afford'. By this definition it makes no sense to cut expenditure on anything we are currently doing.

The dominance of the accountancy paradigm in contemporary debate, perhaps due to its simplicity compared to the paradigm of

> economics, does threaten the possibility of unnecessary constraint on the real economy, specifically arising in socially damaging austerity. Economics challenges accountancy's call for a balanced government budget.

Managing the Economy by the Price of Money—Monetary Policy via the Interest Rate

The primacy of monetary policy derives from the turn to monetarism in economic theory attributed to Milton Friedman and Anna Schwartz,[3] fired by a political kick back against Keynesian government-oriented fiscal policy. The irrational and invalid claim used to support this switch to monetary against fiscal policy was that Keynesian policy had failed at the time of the 1970s OPEC price hike. Politically, monetarism privileged private sector stimulation of the economy over the public sector.

Monetary policy initially sought to control the economy via the quantity of money in circulation, following the 'quantity theory of money'. But commercial bank money creation and elastic credit cards made this impossible. Hence the shift to try to control the quantity of money by its price, the interest rate, a very neoclassical solution.

Since its independence in 1998, the Bank of England (BoE) has been mandated to achieve a 2% inflation target by the sole tool of the interest rate, intended to determine demand in the economy. Raising the interest rate is expected to constrain demand, thus containing inflation if this resulted from excess demand. The simplicity of the underlying monetary theory that an economy can be managed by the price of money is rarely questioned. In reality, the interest rate has both weak and contrary effects on inflation. Consumer disposable income may only be affected with a lag where people hold fixed rate mortgages. People may supplement any lost disposable income by drawing from savings, taking loans, or increasing working hours. The interest rate is powerless against exogenous imported inflation, such as the 1970s OPEC price rise and recent global supply shortages resulting from reduced Chinese production following the Covid pandemic, and the effects of the war in Ukraine.

Worse, interest rate hikes may actually raise inflation through their effect on business costs and investment decisions. The exchange rate is likely to inflate, causing lower import prices, but higher export prices with adverse balance of trade effects. Such counter-inflationary policy focuses exclusively on suppressing demand, rather than on increasing supply and productivity. This would rather require investment which is deterred by high interest rates. Reduced demand itself will also deter investment, yielding a downward vicious circle. Current 2024 dominant service sector inflation requires yet more investment in service sector automation, not increased interest rates. Even monetarists accepted the limit of their interest rate tool when, after the 2007/8 crisis, the economy needed stimulus, and interest rates were considered to be at their minimum, the so-called zero lower bound. Hence the resort to Quantitative Easing analysed below.

Debt Funding in the Private Sector

The current monetary system and associated monetary policy fund both private sector investment and government capital expenditure extensively by debt. Commercial banks create money to extend loans to businesses. Banks apply strict criteria to these loans, requiring a profitable business plan with robust risk assessment, and a likely equity contribution to the investment project. Banks now widely apply enhanced post-crisis conditions that the existing business profitability is sufficient to cover the interest payments on the development loan, and that existing business net assets fully cover loan value. With these conditions, banking becomes risk free.

This post-crisis enhanced conditionality means that commercial banks only lend to established businesses, and not to new start-ups who lack existing profit and net assets to qualify for a loan. This substantially restricts growth in the supply side of the economy, both in investment and production, creating inflation in sectors where supply becomes relatively scarce. The conditions are one source of under-investment in the UK economy, and need reform to allow bank funding of start-ups. But currently, given fulfilment of these conditions, commercial banks then have the extraordinary and unique privilege of creating money to advance the loan, earning an interest rate differential, as well as full seigniorage, which is high given that the money is produced electronically at zero marginal cost. There is a strong a-priori case for taxation of this seigniorage, which is arguably a public right.

Debt Funding in the Public Sector

Meanwhile, due to the prohibition on central banks creating money to directly fund government expenditure set out above, government funds its capital expenditure by borrowing. It incurs debt raised by the sale of its bonds, known as gilts in the UK and Treasuries in the US, to institutions such as pension funds, insurance companies, stockbrokers, rich individuals, and, again curiously, to foreign central banks (whilst not to its own central bank), who are allowed unique access to the primary market for bonds operated by the Debt Management Office (DMO). The myth is that the debt represented by these bonds will be repaid. Following Keynes's advice, governments may operate deficit budgets and accumulate debt expected to be repaid in future years of budget surplus.

But the system has not worked in this way. Instead, governments have racked up cumulative debts equal to or greater than the total annual GDP, and the trend is ever upwards, as shown in Fig. 1.

Figure 1: Debt has risen inexorably over time as a percentage of GDP[4]

The debt/GDP ratio has proved to be extremely fluid, flexible, and apparently arbitrary, not subject to any objective constraint. The 60% debt/GDP ratio set in the Maastricht Treaty for EU states has been well breached as many countries operate with a 100% ratio, or in the extreme case of Japan with a ratio of 254% (Fig. 2).

Figure 2: The debt/GDP ratio shows an extremely wide range, from 25% in Estonia to 254% in Japan, indicating that its level is almost arbitrary and not a binding constraint[5]

Fig 1 Debt/GDP for selected countries 1950-2022

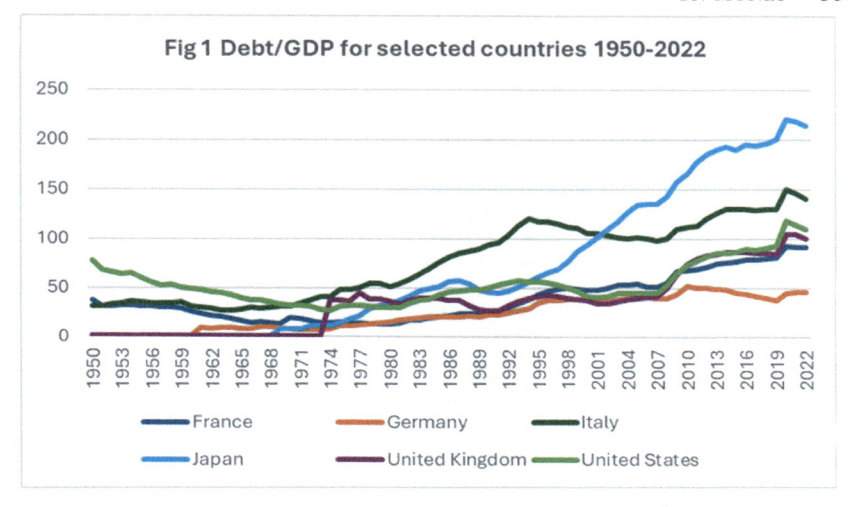

Source IMF Central Government Debt, www.imf.org/external/datamapper/ CG_DEBT_GDP@GDD/CHN/FRA/DEU/ITA/JPN/GBR/USA

Fig 2 Debt/GDP ratios OECD countries 2022

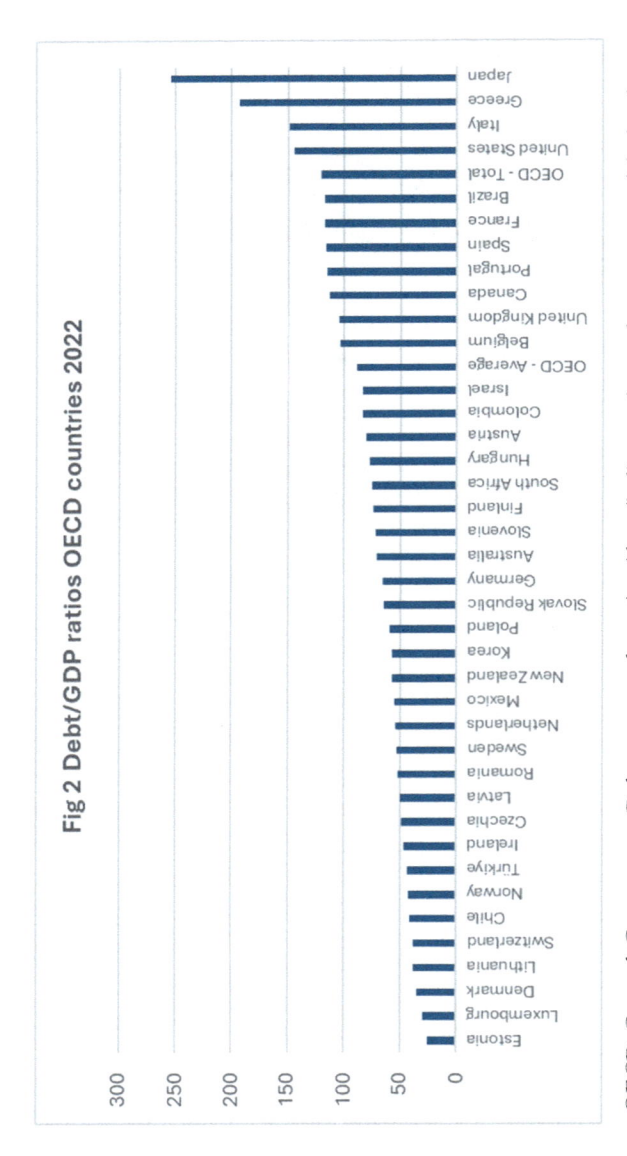

Source OECD General Government Debt www.oecd.org/en/data/indicators/general-government-debt.html

Such 'debts' are mythical in that they can never be repaid. No economy can repay a debt of 100% of its annual GDP, meaning that most debt reaching maturity is rolled over into new debt. These high levels of debt do however impose substantial interest costs on the economy, more so if interest rates rise to counter inflation.

More seriously, debt eventually reaches some arbitrary ceiling at which governments feel constrained to impose austerity policy with the result of massive social harm, and an economy operating at less than potential full employment. Intermediate government financial balances act as the constraint on the economy rather than real resource availability. The tail is now wagging the dog.

A frequent worry is that debt incurred by the present generation is passed on as a repayment liability to future generations. We need to rethink the nature of debt, just as we have had to rethink the nature of money. This is particularly true of inter-generational concepts of debt. Real resources, for example the land, labour, capital equipment, and raw material required to build a hospital, are not borrowed from future generations. It's therefore an unnecessary and damaging practice to render this expenditure as debt in financial terms, and to create a burden for future generations financially when none exists in reality. Transfers from one generation to the next can only be of positive assets, for example of infrastructure and technology, or of depletion of resources and contamination of the environment.

The large question is whether these national debts are necessarily so, or whether alternative definitions of money creation, other than as debt, would have been possible, and are possible for the future.

Quantitative Easing

Quantitative Easing (QE) was overlayed onto this debt-fuelled system. QE was itself an unconventional money policy at its inception in 2009 in response to the economic crisis. Its familiar purpose was to stimulate the post-crisis economy when further reducing interest rates below their 'zero lower bound' was rejected due to an aversion to negative interest rates, and/or considered likely ineffective due to liquidity traps, defined as the point when bonds and money are perfect substitutes. The chosen mechanism of central bank purchase of government debt in the secondary market aimed to increase bond and other asset prices, thus lowering yields, specifically the long-term interest rate, hence stimulating credit growth. At its peak, the Bank of England held £875bn of UK government debt. The process is set out on the BoE web site,[6] together with claims for its efficacy and a rejection of challenges that QE led to inequality. Other reviews[7] have questioned BoE's complacency on the effectiveness of QE in stimulating the economy and avoiding increased inequality. In a working paper of the European Central Bank, 'Fifty shades of QE: comparing findings of central bankers and academics',[8] Brian Fabo, Martina Jančoková, Elisabeth Kempf, and Ľuboš Pástor claim that the impact of QE is reported more favourably by central banks, than by independent academic researchers, and that central bank staff reporting favourable QE outcomes enjoy enhanced career prospects. Central bank staff are often constrained by top management from discussing QE or other central bank policies due to a fear of 'spooking' the markets. This means that key aspects of monetary policy cannot be freely discussed and debated in the public domain, which has reduced the transparency and accountability of central banks. It is unfortunate that the psychology of financial markets has become the dominant factor in the current structure of monetary policy. Evaluations of the effect of QE on GDP tend to converge to a cumulative effect of a meagre 0.5%.

Challenging QE

A first challenge is whether the zero lower bound theory of a minimum interest rate holds true. A European Central Bank (ECB) paper[9] claims to the contrary that negative interest rates can stimulate the economy. Whilst households can withdraw cash to avoid negative interest rates, businesses are unable to, and so are likely to switch funds to investment. Negative interest rates therefore do offer an alternative to QE.

The more urgent current challenge in late 2024 is the cost QE now imposes on public finances, due to the recent rise in the interest rate. To understand this impact, it is necessary to set out the detail of the transactions undertaken by BoE to effect QE. As BoE says, QE has been implemented by BoE buying government bonds, i.e. government debt, in the secondary market, from bondholders like pension funds and insurance companies.

Important Detail

A detailed but important challenge to the system is that BoE is prohibited from buying UK government debt in the primary market[10] auction managed by the Debt Management Office (DMO). At a time when BoE is known to be making massive bond purchases, traders in that primary auction therefore stand to make very substantial profit from onward selling to BoE, at low/zero risk, which could be regarded as scandalous. In their 2016 Bank for International Settlements Paper,[11] Francis Breedon and Philip Turner estimate these transaction costs at 0.5% of the QE amount, which if applied to the total UK QE programme, amounts to £4.4bn. Their paper exposes the scope for price manipulation by traders in the primary bond auction, for which one trader was fined £662,700 by the Financial Conduct Authority for its trade on 10 October 2011. An alternative is therefore to allow BoE to purchase bonds directly from DMO, a move which collapses to direct money financing of government expenditure.

The method by which BoE buys a bond in the secondary market is also of crucial importance. When BoE buys a bond from a pension fund, since the pension fund is not permitted to hold an account with BoE, the only way it is currently able to do this is by creating 'reserves' in the pension fund's commercial bank. These reserves are created digitally, literally from nothing. The commercial bank then credits the pension fund's deposit account, and the transaction is complete.

A very significant point is that BoE agrees to pay the prevailing rate of interest on these reserves it has created with commercial banks for its QE bond purchases. The system is an accident waiting to happen. Except that this accident was foreseeable, at least as a strong possibility, when the very same BoE decided on the need to increase the interest rate to constrain macroeconomic inflation.

A further significant point is that BoE decided, or it could be argued needed, to purchase long-term fixed interest bonds—a detail with profound future repercussions.

Adverse Outcomes

Two very adverse effects then kicked in. Firstly, BoE's decision to purchase long-term fixed interest bonds means that subsequent high interest rates applied by BoE to counter inflation, reduced the value of

BoE's bond holding, since the price of bonds is inversely related to the interest rate. Estimates of the size of this loss[12] vary between £130bn and £230bn,[13] which is not necessarily incurred until maturity of the bond, unless a programme of bond sales, known as Quantitative Tightening (QT) is implemented. In February 2022, the Monetary Policy Committee (MPC) of BoE did decide to implement QT and has since reduced its holding of bonds from a peak of £875bn to some £700bn. BoE has incurred a very large but unreported loss on the sale of this £175bn tranche of bonds. QT has essentially re-created net government debt since the debt is then owed to the private sector, and not to its own central bank.

Secondly, the decision to pay interest on the reserves created with commercial banks to purchase bonds for QE, left BoE paying 5.25% on the reserves, against which it gained only around 2% on the long-term fixed interest bonds it purchased. This amounts to an annual loss of some £23bn. BoE was then in a cleft stick. Either it would incur a capital loss if it sells its QE bonds, or it would incur a revenue loss if it continued to hold them.

Summary of QE's Dysfunctionality

It is hard not to conclude that QE has proved to be extremely dysfunctional. Before moving on to consider alternatives to QE, we can summarise its major points of failure as

- BoE is not allowed to purchase bonds in the primary DMO auction, thus hugely enriching intermediaries at low/zero risk.
- BoE purchased long-term fixed interest bonds, which then reduced in value due to anti-inflationary interest rate rises.
- BoE funded this by creating reserves with commercial banks on which it pays variable rate interest, creating huge losses for BoE, whilst generating huge unearned profit for commercial banks.
- Because the UK government Treasury indemnifies BoE against all such losses, the losses are then incurred by government, hugely affecting its budget and expenditure.
- BoE failed to publish any risk testing of its QE strategy for discussion in the public domain, even against the risk of interest rate rises which BoE itself controls.

The extent of this dysfunctionality calls into question the widely supported independence of BoE. In reality, the purchase of £875bn government debt may well not have been carried out entirely independently of government. Total independence implies a lack of accountability. If totally independent, then BoE must assume total responsibility for the outcomes of its actions. The opposite is in fact the case, because BoE is granted indemnity on any loss it makes which is passed on to HM Treasury, i.e. paid from public funds. Responsibility has to be defined to some other agency. Officially, BoE reports to the Parliamentary Treasury Committee, but it is doubtful that this committee has the technical ability and necessary resource to oversee BoE effectively. Given the huge social and economic impact of its actions, specifically the way it conducted QE, there is a strong case for BoE independence to be qualified by a line of clearly defined public accountability, and/or for its indemnity to be reconsidered.

Alternatives to QE

A range of tactical and strategic alternatives therefore presents.
For past learning

- negative interest rates could have tested the reality of the zero lower bound theory
- BoE should have purchased other than long-term fixed interest bonds
- BoE should have been allowed to purchase bonds from DMO directly.

For future practice

- BoE should not pay variable rate interest on the tranche of reserves it created with commercial banks to fund QE.
- Some part of government expenditure should be funded by direct money financing, not by debt.

Taking these in turn, as an IMF review[14] reports, real interest rates have often been negative, but negative nominal interest rates have been a component of recent monetary policy, both in the EU and in Japan.[15]

There is a case for inclusion of negative nominal interest rates in BoE's toolkit in the UK.

The UK Treasury does not issue variable rate bonds, so that BoE's main alternative choices in bond purchase would have been short-term bonds, or inflation index-linked bonds, known as 'linkers'. There is some indication that short-term bond issuance would have achieved the policy objective of reduction of the long-term interest rate[16]. The problem for BoE buying linkers, is that, since their yield is inflation linked, it is not clear that an increase in their price would have reduced their interest rate in the way needed for BoE's QE objective. Once inflation did bite, their nominal yield would rise, but by definition their real yield would remain constant. Whether the increase in their yield would have matched the increase in BoE variable interest payments on commercial bank QE reserves requires more detailed study and modelling. This suggests that there is no ideal bond for BoE purchase in a QE scheme, making initial direct money financing the preferable option.

The proposal for BoE to cease variable interest payments on commercial bank reserves, or to tier these reserves into tranches of differential interest rate payment, has received substantial recent attention in an extensive 2022 IFS paper by Paul Tucker,[17] an FT article by Chris Giles,[18] and a CEPS paper by Paul de Grauwe and Yuemei Ji.[19] Commercial banks are receiving a margin on the 5.25% BoE is currently paying them (September 2024) on the £700bn remaining QE reserves BoE created for them, against any deposit interest the commercial bank is paying the original bond holder, for example, the pension fund. This amounts to a huge profit for doing nothing. Supporters of BoE variable rate interest payment on these reserves claim any reduction amounts to a tax on banks, or violates the initial agreement with the banks. Respondents argue that if it is a tax, it's levied on an unearned unjustified gain. Moreover, the fundamental transaction is between the BoE and the pension fund for the bond sale. The commercial bank is only an intermediary. The pension fund is not driven by the interest it foresees earning on the proceeds of the bond sale, but i) on the value of the bond sale itself and ii) on alternative investment of the bond sale proceeds, for example in equities. If historic commitments to pay variable rate interest on QE reserves cannot be reversed, then no further such agreements should be part of any future QE.

Allowing BoE to purchase bonds from DMO directly would have removed the intermediary profit objection of restricting BoE to the secondary market. However, this would make it all the clearer that government debt held by its own central bank amounts to zero net debt. Both the interest and the principal of any such debt are owed by the government to its own central bank! This is equivalent to, and collapses to, the final proposal for direct money financing of government expenditure, avoiding debt funding.

IMPLICATIONS OF QE FOR THE REDESIGN OF MONETARY POLICY

This is the most significant implication and learning from QE, i.e., that when a central bank purchases its own government debt, and is itself owned by the same government, or in the case of the US Federal Reserve, is required to pay any surpluses to the US Treasury, then this amounts to zero net debt. It is equivalent to direct money financing of government expenditure, and has therefore demonstrated its feasibility. It has been arrived at by a complex route with serious dysfunctionality, all of which would be avoided by explicit overt direct money financing.

CALLS FOR REFORM

History has seen many calls for reform of the monetary system and of monetary policy. We now focus on contemporary calls for reform in the light of the lessons learned from QE and QT.

Jaromir Benes and Michael Kumhof in their 2012 IMF paper 'The Chicago Plan Revisited',[20] revive the 1930s Chicago Plan of Henry Simons and Irving Fisher. The proposal is

- withdrawal of commercial bank licence to create money, thus avoiding credit cycles
- requiring 100% reserves of government issued money for all bank deposits
- allowing direct money financing of government expenditure by central bank creation of debt-free sovereign money
- constraining private sector investment by government money aggregate quantity control.

These measures are claimed to result in the reduction of economic cycles, the elimination of runs on banks, the reduction of government debt, and the reduction of private sector debt. The proposed system would shift the licence to create money from commercial banks to the central bank, thus correcting the current inequity whereby commercial banks gain seigniorage and earn interest by creating money which then morphs into debt assumed by government to fund its expenditure. In this system, government assumes a monopoly on money creation. Benes and Kumhof report extensive econometric mathematical modelling of their proposal which demonstrates its viability.

Joseph Huber in his 'Sovereign Money'[21] similarly advocates government monopoly on money creation. The proposal was put to a democratic referendum in Switzerland in June 2018. The Swiss National Bank opposed the proposal on the grounds that the national bank lacks expertise and resources to manage private sector personal and business loans, and did not favour nationalisation of commercial banks to achieve the objective. The German Bundesbank also opposed the proposal which was defeated by a 75% majority of votes in the national referendum.

Adair Turner in his 2015 IMF paper, 'The Case for Monetary Finance—An Essentially Political Issue'[22] argues that direct money financing of government expenditure faces no technical obstacle, and is merely a political question. Turner shows that not only is money financing feasible and unproblematic, but is also the most effective policy tool to achieve a demand stimulus, when compared to debt-financed expenditure, and to QE. It is moreover a controllable tool and can be scaled and calibrated to avoid inflation. He accepts that his analysis operates in a neo-Keynesian world with potentially less than full employment, where aggregate demand may be deficient. His analysis focussing on achieving a needed demand stimulus, can equally apply as an argument against austerity. He points out that QT will generate a future debt financing burden, and so proposes making QE permanent with irredeemable zero interest coupons. In order to avoid bank credit multipliers applying to any direct money financing, Turner proposes zero interest commercial bank reserves at the central bank which he accepts is a tax on commercial bank credit. To avoid government profligacy, Monetary Policy Committee approval should be required for tranches of direct money financing. Turner regards direct money financing as a one-off policy tool and doubts its permanent relevance.

Gerald Holtham in his 2021 paper 'Monetary policy and the value of Public Debt',[23] published by NIESR, also argues that commercial banks should be required to lodge interest-free reserves with the Bank of England by fiat.

The school of 'Modern Monetary Theory' argues that government expenditure should be constrained by real resource availability and not by an artificial limit on government deficit financing. According to MMT, government deficits will accumulate into debt which is matched by surpluses in the private and foreign sectors of the economy. This observation, which is due to Francis Cripps and Wynne Godley, is tautologically true, but as a post-hoc identity. Variation in any one of these three balances does not directly cause exact, equal, and immediate variation in the other two balances, but does cause an iteration of the macroeconomy to reach a new equilibrium where the three balances again sum to zero, but at a different level.

I have argued for debt-free sovereign money in my 2020 'Basic Income and Sovereign Money—The Alternative to Economic Crisis and Austerity Policy'.[24]

UK national debt now (2024) stands at £2.6tn, representing cumulative government expenditure. If a portion of that same historic expenditure, say £600bn, had instead been funded by direct money finance, then

- Public sector debt and its interest financing cost would be reduced.
- Austerity would be avoided as calls to limit public sector debt or the debt/GDP ratio would diminish.
- The economy could operate at full employment.
- There would have been no inflationary or any other effect on the downstream economy, since the expenditure implemented would be the same as actually happened.
- The only effect would be that pension funds and insurance companies would hold the additional £600bn not used to buy bonds over the years. This would certainly remove the threat of foreclosure and bankruptcy via LDI hedge policies on their gilt holdings for pension funds. It would also enable increased investment in UK equities by pension funds which is a current target of government policy. The research question then is how pension funds and insurance companies would have likely allocated the £600bn funding differently.

Reform Proposals Diagrammatically

The reforms set out above can be represented in visual diagrams.

The standard system **before QE** can be shown as (HSBC is used for convenience as a typical commercial bank) (Fig. 3).

Figure 3: Debt funding of government expenditure

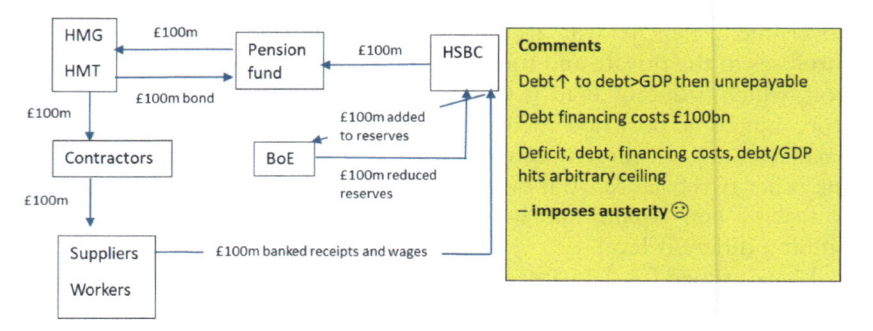

Comments

Debt ↑ to debt>GDP then unrepayable

Debt financing costs £100bn

Deficit, debt, financing costs, debt/GDP hits arbitrary ceiling

– **imposes austerity** ☹

Overlaying QE (blue lines) onto this system shows as (Fig. 4)

Figure 4: Quantitative Easing after debt funding of government expenditure

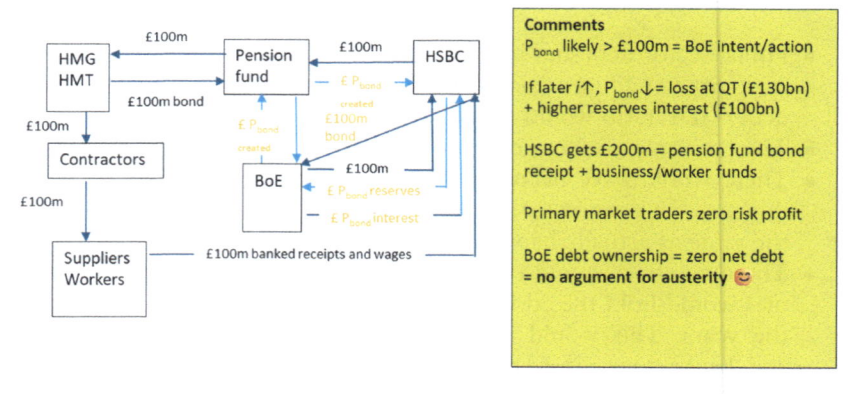

Comments

P_{bond} likely > £100m = BoE intent/action

If later i↑, P_{bond}↓ = loss at QT (£130bn) + higher reserves interest (£100bn)

HSBC gets £200m = pension fund bond receipt + business/worker funds

Primary market traders zero risk profit

BoE debt ownership = zero net debt = no argument for austerity ☺

Adair Turner and Gerald Holtham's proposal for commercial banks to lodge interest-free reserves at the Bank of England removes the payment of interest by the Bank of England from the above diagram and is then shown as (Fig. 5)

Figure 5: Proposals for central bank interest-free reserves

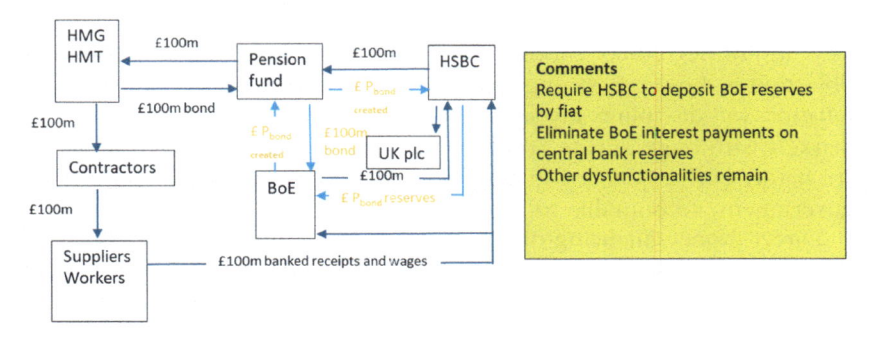

Comments
Require HSBC to deposit BoE reserves by fiat
Eliminate BoE interest payments on central bank reserves
Other dysfunctionalities remain

And finally, the proposal for direct money financing argued by Adair Turner described as debt-free sovereign money in my work is (Fig. 6)

Figure 6: Direct money financing of government expenditure

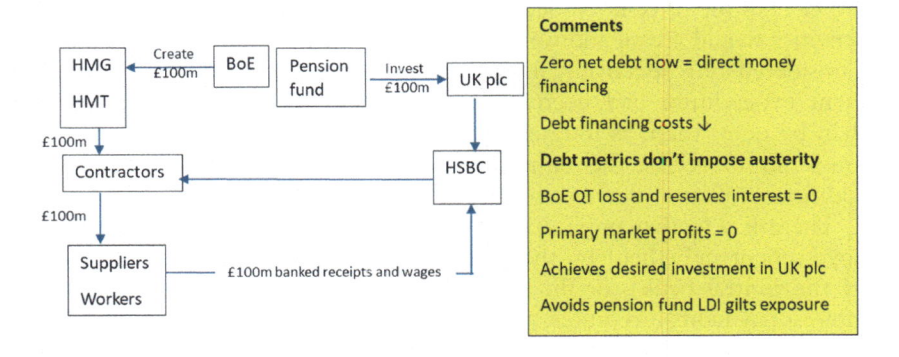

Comments
Zero net debt now = direct money financing
Debt financing costs ↓
Debt metrics don't impose austerity
BoE QT loss and reserves interest = 0
Primary market profits = 0
Achieves desired investment in UK plc
Avoids pension fund LDI gilts exposure

In Favour of Direct Money Financing of Government Expenditure

Adair Turner's 2015 IMF paper[25] cited above is a seminal contribution on direct money financing of government expenditure. Turner shows conclusively that there is no technical obstacle to monetary finance, which is purely a political question, writing 'on close inspection, all apparent technical objections to monetary finance dissolve. There is no doubt that monetary finance is technically feasible and that wise fiscal and monetary authorities could choose just the "right" amount'. This political objection is, however, strong, due to fears of government profligacy. But inflation will discipline any such tendency to profligacy. Unelected bond markets with huge private profit drivers, or an independent central bank, are hardly better qualified guardians of the public purse, than an elected government, accountable to its electorate.

Direct money financing of government expenditure would reduce the amount of government debt in the economy. Effectively, the £875bn peak holding of government debt by BoE reduced net government debt by that amount. With direct money financing, the need for QE with all its dysfunctionality never arises. The policy can be justified for both regular government expenditure and occasional stimulus. Concerns about inflation can be addressed in two ways. First, with interest paying money, any additional money supply would drive up the interest rate on money rather than the price level. Second, direct money financing for productive activities would create additional supply to match the additional demand. Considered retrospectively, if exactly the same £875bn historic government expenditure had been funded by direct money financing rather than by debt, then, as long as pension funds and others holding higher funds did not release them into direct demand, there would have been no additional inflation downstream in the economy.

There is a further implication of huge social importance. The level of government debt held by the private sector (which excludes debt held by the central bank), or the debt/GDP ratio it implies, or the level of interest payments it requires, are often used as an indicator of affordability of government expenditure, and as an argument to necessitate austerity. The damaging social consequences of austerity are well documented, as cited above in the Joseph Rowntree Foundation's 2024 Poverty report.[26] Keynes's claim that 'anything we can actually do, we can afford' has to be true, and obviates any debt-driven case for cuts in existing social welfare programmes. Funding is available. The constraint to government expenditure is real resource availability, not the intermediate variable of government financial balances. There is a magical money tree—obviously so. The responsible constraint is resource availability and, relatedly, inflation.

Direct money financing would reduce the purchase of government debt by pension funds and insurance companies, thereby allowing them to instead favour alternative investments, for example UK equities, to the benefit of the UK economy. Furthermore, excessive holdings of gilts can generate liquidity crises such as experienced during the LDI crisis, and can even threaten pension fund failure.

Conclusion—In Favour of Direct Money Financing of Government Expenditure

The conclusion is that direct money financing is by far preferable to QE with its extensive dysfunctionality. Adair Turner's proposal for direct money financing, and Paul Tucker's proposal for tiering BoE reserves at commercial banks are important key proposals. They have been swept under the table. They deserve serious consideration.

References

1. Michael Kumhof et al. *Central Bank Money: Liability, Asset or Equity of the Nation?*, 2020. https://papers.ssrn.com/sol3/papers.cfm?abstract_id=3730608
2. John Maynard Keynes, *The General Theory of Employment, Interest, and Money* (London: MacMillan, 1936).
3. Milton Friedman and Anna Schwartz, *A Monetary History of the United States, 1867–1960* (Princeton: Princeton University Press, 1963).
4. International Monetary Fund, 'Government Debt-to-GDP Data', 2024, www.imf.org/external/datamapper/CG_DEBT_GDP@GDD/CHN/FRA/DEU/ITA/JPN/GBR/USA.
5. OECD, 'General Government Debt', www.oecd.org/en/data/indicators/general-government-debt.html.
6. Bank of England, 'Quantitative Easing: How It Works', www.bankofengland.co.uk/monetary-policy/quantitative-easing#:~:text=QE%20involves%20us%20buying%20bonds,895%20billion%20worth%20of%20bonds.
7. Positive Money, 'How Quantitative Easing Works', https://positivemoney.org/archive/how-quantitative-easing-works/
8. Brian Fabo, Martina Jančoková, Elisabeth Kempf, Luboš Pástor, 'Fifty Shades of QE: Comparing Findings of Central Bankers and

Academics', ECB (2021) www.ecb.europa.eu/pub/pdf/scpwps/ecb.wp2584~004629c8e7.en.pdf
9. European Central Bank, 'The Zero Lower Bound and Negative Interest Rates', 2020. www.ecb.europa.eu/pub/pdf/scpwps/ecb.wp2289~1a3c04db25.en.pdf
10. UK Parliament, 'Bank of England Act 1998', 1998, https://www.legislation.gov.uk/ukpga/1998/11/section/14.
11. Francis Breedon and Philip Turner, 'On the Transactions Costs of Quantitative Easing', Bank for International Settlements (2016) www.bis.org/publ/work571.pdf
12. Financial Times, 'Bank of England's Quantitative Tightening is a Leap in the Dark', 2024. www.ft.com/content/d65ccaa7-e12b-4d9a-a132-11180d39f891
13. Financial Times. 'The Bank of England Is Misusing Its Fiscal Powers' (2024) www.ft.com/content/5209be99-3f6b-4ba3-b3f3-49b544f71c28
14. International Monetary Fund (IMF), 'What Are Negative Interest Rates?', 2020.
15. World Economic Forum, 'Japan Ends Negative Interest Rates: Economy and Monetary Policy', 2024.
16. Francis Breedon and Philip Turner, 'On the Transactions Costs of Quantitative Easing', Bank for International Settlements (2016) www.bis.org/publ/work571.pdf
17. P. Tucker, 'Quantitative Easing: Monetary Policy Implementation and Public Finances', 2022, https://ifs.org.uk/publications/quantitative-easing-monetary-policy-implementation-and-public-finances.
18. C. Giles, 'Towards Monetary Policies That Do Not Subsidise Banks', 2024, https://www.ft.com/content/2fbe1549-33d4-472a-9cc0-f7791459d3a9.
19. P. De Grauwe and Y. Ji, 'Towards Monetary Policies That Do Not Subsidise Banks', 2023, https://cdn.ceps.eu/wp-content/uploads/2023/07/Towards-monetary-policies-that-do-not-subsidise-banks_July2023.pdf.
20. Jaromir Benes and Michael Kumhof, 'The Chicago Plan Revisited', 2012.
21. Joseph Huber, *Sovereign Money: Beyond Reserve Banking* (Springer, 2017).

22. Adair Turner, 'The Case for Monetary Finance—An Essentially Political Issue' (International Monetary Fund (IMF) Working Paper, 2015).
23. G. Holtham, *Monetary Policy and the Value of Public Debt* (Welsh Economic Challenge Paper, 2021), https://www.welsheconomicchallenge.com/wp-content/uploads/2021/02/Monetary_policy_the_value_of_Public_Debt.pdf.
24. G. Crocker, *Basic Income and Sovereign Money—The Alternative to Economic Crisis and Austerity Policy* (Springer, 2020).
25. Adair Turner, 'The Case for Monetary Finance—An Essentially Political Issue'. www.imf.org/external/np/res/seminars/2015/arc/pdf/adair.pdf.
26. Joseph Rowntree Foundation, 'UK Poverty 2024: The Essential Guide to Understanding Poverty in the UK'.

On Technology

Abstract This chapter explores the integration of technology into economic theory, focussing on its impact on labour, production, and income distribution. Technological advancements initially displace labour through automation but subsequently augment employment in new industries and roles, ultimately increasing productivity and consumption. Technology thus reduces labour's share of income while generating new economic opportunities. This leads to wage inequality and income inadequacy, particularly in low-income households. Increased non-labour income, such as universal basic income, and increased targeted welfare benefits with reduced conditionality become essential.

Keywords Automation · Labour displacement · Labour augmentation · Productivity · Mass production · Income inequality · Economies of scale · Universal basic income (UBI)

Integrating Technology and Economics
Towards a Model

Technology is fundamental to economic theory, but largely excluded from it. Technology drives

- **consumption** by creating a plethora of new and constantly redefined products and services
- **production** by radically altering the capital/labour production function, raising productivity
- **distribution**, by shifting retail sales online, and automating warehousing and logistics
- **employment** by quantity, type, skill-level, and wage
- **income** by level, distribution, and composition between labour and non-labour income
- **market transactions and outcomes** by Internet information flows and transactions processing
- **standard of living** via productivity increase and real price decrease, further driving consumption.

Technology can both displace and augment labour.

Technology as automation initially displaces labour. In this first round effect, the labour share of GDP, and aggregate wage in the economy will decline. In a market economy, such cost reduction would be a necessary driver and outcome of the investment in automation. Cost reduction therefore inevitably results from automation. However, automation also simultaneously augments retained labour by requiring higher skilled labour at a higher wage which then increases aggregate wage in the economy. But this increase may well be less than the aggregate wage reduction caused by displaced labour.

The second round effect is that, through the huge economies of scale achieved by mass production, increased productivity reduces product price. This stimulates demand, production, and employment. It can be a very large effect, historically contributing to enormous economic growth. It does then require further investment and 'capital deepening'. In this second round, technology is labour augmenting.

Thirdly, technology creates entirely new products and services. This is clearly labour augmenting and represents a huge part of increased GDP.

Finally, technology creates its own industry sector. R&D creates extensive high-wage employment.

In summary, technology

- displaces labour in initial automation
- augments labour retained in higher wage automated jobs
- augments labour by the growth of production resulting from the unit cost reduction obtained from the economies of scale of mass production, and the consequent increased consumption of lower priced products
- augments labour in production of new products and services
- augments labour in the technology sector itself.

This immediately suggests that the labour augmenting effect of technology far outweighs its labour displacement effect. The same people who are displaced labour may in fact often become augmented labour. This has undoubtedly been the case historically in the economy since the industrial revolution. It will continue to be the case as long as society increases its consumption of the increased output of existing products, and the total output of new products made available by technology. At some point, society faces the choice of whether to take the benefits of technology in extra consumption, or in reduced labour and increased leisure. This total process does not leave everyone unambiguously better off. Inequality increases both between displaced and augmented labour, and within employed labour.

The concern is that whenever technology reduces the aggregate labour share, aggregate demand, and household incomes, then an increase in non-labour or social welfare income becomes necessary, either as targeted conditional welfare benefits, or universal basic income. If augmented labour exceeds displaced labour, then the aggregate effect is to maintain aggregate demand in the economy, but this leaves an important distributional issue between unemployment and employment, and within employment. The analysis of the income section of this book above shows that such inequality is a clear, continuing, and substantial phenomenon. Moreover recent academic research reported below suggests that, more recently, labour has suffered greater displacement than augmentation. Empirical observation of in-work poverty, low pay, 'bullshit' jobs, and rising household debt, all indicate that work and wage fail to generate adequate household income for low-income quintile households. Indeed, an alternative explanation of the 2007 economic crisis is that the crisis resulted from deficient aggregate demand with excessive household debt compensating for the reduction in labour income.

The policy implication is therefore for a focus on income rather than employment, with a need for increased non-labour social welfare income. A secondary discussion then focusses on whether non-labour income is best targeted and therefore conditional or universal.

To exemplify the various effects of technology on the economy, we consider automation in the weaving industry, alongside the initial creation first of car technology, followed by mobile phone technology (Table 1). The techno-economic process is

Table 1 The techno-economic process

Step	Technology	GDP	Employment	Aggregate labour income	Economic dynamic		
					R&D	Capital Investment	Capital Deepening*
1	Create automated loom	↑	↑	↑			
2	Deploy automated loom	=	↓	↓			
3	Expand cloth output	↑	↑	↑			
4	Create car	↑	↑	↑			
5	Invest car production	↑	↑	↑			
6	Produce cars	↑	↑	↑			
7	Create car production robots	↑	↑	↑			
8	Deploy automated car production	=	↓	↓			
9	Increase car output	↑	↑	↑			
10	Create mobile phone	↑	↑	↑			
11	Deploy mobile phone	↑	↑	↑			
12	Create mobile phone apps	↑	↑	↑			
13	Deploy mobile phone apps	↑	↑ and ↓	↑ or ↓ ?		Systems investment	

*Demand increases as economies of scale from mass production reduce product cost and hence product price

In each of the steps where a new technology and/or product is created (steps 1, 4, 7, 10, 12), R&D, design, and product development are needed, all of which raise GDP, create employment, and increase aggregate labour income. Technology development can result from entrepreneurial 'animal spirits', academic scientific research, corporate technology strategies, and government technology policies.

Where automation technology is deployed to maintain current output (steps 2 and 8), GDP initially remains constant, but employment and aggregate labour income reduce, which is likely to have second round multiplier effects of reducing GDP.

As automation, through the economies of scale of mass production, reduces product price and stimulates price-elastic demand increase, 'capital deepening' then takes place to increase output (steps 3, 6, 11, 13), then GDP, employment, and aggregate labour income will initially increase. But mobile apps may well reduce employment in retail and service sectors. An important factor in this phase is that the price of capital goods themselves reduces through their own mass production, giving further cost advantage to incentivise more capital deepening.

Empirical data on reducing aggregate labour income and deficient household income suggests that the loss of aggregate labour income in steps 2 and 8 exceeds the gains in aggregate labour income of all other processes of techno-economic growth, but specifically for low-income households. This concurs with Acemoglu and Restrepo's (2019) findings below.

Literature Review

There is considerable evolution and debate in the academic literature on the labour displacement and labour augmenting effects of technological automation. David Autor and Daron Acemoglu are amongst the leading authors in the field.

Acemoglu in 'Labor- and Capital-Augmenting Technical Change' (2003)[1] claims that the labour share of GDP is constant in the long run, and that all technical change is labour augmenting. Both of these claims are challenged in later development of the literature, which finds widely declining labour shares of GDP, with the labour displacement effect of automation predominant over its labour augmentation effect. The assumption of a Cobb–Douglas production function with an elasticity of substitution between capital and labour equal to 1 is key. The maths in the paper is technical and complex, and so difficult to assimilate or to challenge.

But in a later paper, 'Automation and New Tasks: How Technology Displaces and Reinstates Labor' (2019),[2] Acemoglu and Restrepo distinguish labour displacement effects of technology as 'automation', versus labour reinstatement effects of 'new task' technology. They conclude that from 1947 to 1987 in the US economy these were equal, but that over the following 30 years, displacement has outweighed reinstatement. This view is supported by Klump, McAdam, and Willman in 'Factor Substitution and Factor Augmenting Technical Progress in the Us: A Normalized Supply-Side System Approach' (2004).[3]

Acemoglu and Restrepo's proxy measures for automation technology are robot industry penetration, industry share of routine jobs, and the share of firms using automation technology. It's not clear why these are not collinear, or whether their model corrects for multicollinearity. Their proxy measures for new task technology are largely new job titles and occupations. They claim that high-wages incentivise automation, but that new task and product technology development and implementation may slow due to a burn out of ideas, diminishing returns, and a lack of new task labour skills.

A useful overview of the literature is provided by Squicciarini and Staccioli in 'Labour-Saving Technologies and Employment Levels' (2022).[4] Their methodology uses language detection techniques to identify labour saving technology patents from over 6 million patents filed between 1978 and 2019. They find such labour saving patents concentrated in Japan, US, and Italy, with only 25% located in Europe. Japanese robot manufacturers are the dominant player. The labour saving effects of the patents apply to all skill levels, but in aggregate do not generate any reduction in employment shares.

Mann and Püttmann in 'Benign Effects of Automation: New Evidence from Patent Texts' (2018)[5] claim that employment loss from automation is more than compensated by service sector growth. Bessen, 'Automation and Jobs: When Technology Boosts Employment' (2018)[6] shows how automation increases industry employment as the reduced product price generates price-elastic demand, a trend which he then shows diminishes over time due to demand satiation. Dechezleprêtre et al. 'Automating Labor: Evidence From Firm-Level Patent Data' (2019)[7] find that high low-skill wages lead to increased automation, whereas high high-skill wages reduce automation. Acemoglu and Restrepo, 'Robots and Jobs: Evidence from US Labor Markets' (2020),[8] report that every additional robot per thousand workers reduces the employment/population ratio by 0.2%, and wages by 0.42%. Frey and Osborne 'The Future of Employment: How Susceptible are Jobs to Computerisation?' (2013)[9]

estimate that 47% of US employment faces future threats from automation, whilst Arntz, Gregory, and Zierahn, 'The Risk of Automation for Jobs in OECD Countries: A Comparative Analysis' (2016),[10] estimate that only 9% of jobs are at risk from automation in OECD countries, which Nedelkoska and Quintini 'Automation, skills use and training' (2018)[11] estimate at 14%. Georgieff and Milanez 'What happened to jobs at high risk of automation?' (2021)[12] show that for the period 2012–2019, employment growth was lower in jobs at high risk of automation. Staccioli and Virgillito 'Back to the past: the historical roots of labor-saving automation' (2021)[13] track labour saving innovations against GDP growth in the nineteenth century.

David Autor and Anna Salomons, 'Is automation labor-displacing? Productivity growth, employment, and the labor share' Brookings (2018),[14] write 'although automation – whether measured by Total Factor Productivity growth, or instrumented by foreign patent flows, or robot adoption - has not been labour displacing, it has reduced labour's share in value added' (abstract). Labour share had always been assumed constant by economists, and was so in the 1970s, but declined in the 1980/90 s, and has done further since 2000. Loukas Karabarbounis and Brent Neiman, 'The Global Decline of the Labor Share (2013)[15]', show that reduction in the labour share is caused by reduction in the relative price of ICT goods. The main point is that aggregate wage grew less than value added.

William F. Maloney and Carlos Molina, 'Is Automation Labor-Displacing in the Developing Countries, Too?: Robots, Polarization, and Jobs',[16] (2019) show that robots cause labour market polarisation and labour displacement in developed economies, but not in developing economies. Service sector employment fully compensates for manufacturing employment loss in developed economies. Robots create jobs at all levels in developing economies where no operator and assembler jobs previously existed.

Maloney and Molina cite

- Goos, Manning, and Solomons 'Explaining Job Polarization: Routine-Biased Technological Change and Offshoring (2014)[17]' that from 1993 to 2006, middle-income employment reduced in 16 EU countries

- Acemoglu and Restrepo 'Robots And Jobs: Evidence From US Labor Markets' (2017)[18] that US robots reduced employment and wage 1990–2007
- Dauth, 'German Robots – The Impact of Industrial Robots on Workers' (2017)[19] that between 1994 and 2014, German robots reduced manufacturing employment by 23%
- Gregory, Salomons, and Zierahn 'Racing With or Against the Machine? Evidence from Europe' (2016)[20] that in 238 EU regions, routine replacing technological change (RRTC) reduced employment, but service sector employment grew.

Robots reduced employment in China and Mexico, whilst Mexico's exports to the US reduced with US robot deployment.

Industrial robot installations grew through

- 1973–3000
- 2010–1,059,000
- 2019–2,589,000.

In 2018, 73% of all global robot installations were in China, Japan, South Korea, US, and Germany. The main installation sectors were automotive, electrical/electronic, metals, chemicals, and plastics.

Operator and assembler employment reduced with robots, but no wage polarisation was found in 21 developing countries.

Michael Webb 'The Impact of Artificial Intelligence on the Labor Market' (2020),[21] adds the dimension of 'occupation' to Acemoglu and Restrepo's 2018 paper. The main impacts of three sequential phases of automation are that robots affect low-skill jobs, software affects medium skill jobs, whilst artificial intelligence affects high-skill jobs.

Luís Guimarães and Pedro Mazeda Gil, 'Explaining the Labor Share: Automation Vs Labor Market Institutions' (2022),[22] show that since 1987, the fall in the US labour share is better explained by technology and automation than by labour bargaining power. The productivity of automation accelerated significantly from 1987.

Herbert Dawid and Michael Neugart, 'Effects of technological change and automation on industry structure and (wage-)inequality: insights from a dynamic task-based model' (2022),[23] report simulations of experimental economics modelling to explore 'the distributional effects of automation' (p. 36), whereby firms decide to allocate workers or machines to specific tasks.

Their scenarios are differentiated by whether

- firms are in a competitive market or not
- worker skills are homogenous or heterogeneous
- firms face labour bargaining or not
- firms pass benefits to wages or not.

Outcomes show 'how aggregate income balances labour creation and destruction to avoid persistent technological unemployment' (p. 37). But Bertani (2020, 2021) has outcomes with long-term unemployment. Many authors, Dosi, Dawid, Caioni, Hepp, are more concerned with effects on wage distribution, whilst Domini (2022) suggests automation does not cause wage inequality. Dawid and Neugart find wage inequality in-firm rather than inter-firm.

They analyse the effect of automation on

- labour share
- real wage
- employment
- wage distribution.

From a plethora of scenarios, they conclude that the effect of automation is very dependent on a wide range of conditions. In particular, the degree of competition in the sector appears determinative.

Meanwhile, the global consultancy McKinsey[24] in a 2018 presentation report that in 2016, expenditure on artificial intelligence amounted to $15–23bn in the US, $8–12bn in Asia, but only $3–4bn in the EU. A 15% reduction in employment by 2030 from artificial intelligence is predicted to be more than matched by a 21–33% increase in new jobs. Their final conclusion expects full employment enabled by job retraining, with some potential and need for a universal basic income.

The accountancy and consulting firm PWC explores three waves of automation.[25] Their report assesses the main effect of automation on financial services, transport, and health for 29 OECD countries using Frey and Osborne methodology disaggregated by sector, occupation, and educational level. They estimate that automation could add 14% to world

GDP, equal to $15tn. Their results analyse feasibility, not actuality, and don't include offsetting job creation. Frey and Osborne predicted 47% job loss from their binary chop analysis by job, whilst OECD predicted a lower 10% by detailed task analysis. PWC estimate this at 30%. They repeat the challenge to universal basic income proposals as being either too small to be meaningful or too large to be affordable (Section 7.3), and claim that services are less automatable, despite huge recent automation in banking, insurance, ticketing, etc. Their policy recommendation is for education, training, government expenditure, basic income, and a culture of entrepreneurial response to opportunities. Their later 2021 report simply assumes that job creation will equal job displacement, and analyses the distributional effect of job losses.

The OECD[26] report on the labour share in G20 countries shows that labour share and inequality are positively correlated, and that productivity has grown more than the real wage.

The Resolution Foundation report 'Dead End Relationship'[27] finds that UK productivity has fed into real wage, but there has been little growth in productivity. The median real weekly wage in 2018 was £439, 1.8% less than its £447 level in 2004. US output/hour has exceeded pay since 1980, whereas in the UK the difference is less and occurred later from 1990.

In their 2021 book 'The Work of the Future'[28] David Autor, David Mindell, and Elisabeth Reynolds of MIT's 'Task Force on the Work of the Future' conclude that technology is not 'driving us to a jobless future' (p. 135). Rather they focus on the extremely unequal impact of technology adversely affecting low-income workers, specifically so in the US, where low-skill pay is 79% of that in the UK, 74% of Canada's and 57% of Germany's (p. 25). From 1978 to 2016, US output/hour increased by 66%, but production worker pay by only 12% (p. 19). The US labour share of GDP has fallen to 67% from 75% in the 1970s, but more so in sectors using robotics (p. 30). They are optimistic that a historic virtuous combination of technology, full employment, and high wages (p. 4), can persist into the future, because (i) their research into insurance and health, autonomous vehicles, manufacturing and distribution, additive manufacturing sectors (p. 41) shows ambiguous outcomes with 'momentous impacts, unfolding gradually' (p. 75), and (ii) a continuing trend of new job creation since 'most of today's jobs hadn't even been invented in 1940' (p. 7). They expect this to result from 'unforeseen technologies (which) will not necessarily benefit all workers' (p. 135).

To correct the distributional consequences, they propose a combination of vocationally focussed education and training, an increased minimum wage which is comparatively low in the US, increased public R&D, more effective collective bargaining, and more equal labour and capital taxation. They favour their work-centric philosophy over proposals for a universal basic income (p. 102).

Their confidence is uplifting but not well founded. Their empirical report does not cover the widespread closure of staffed high street banks, transportation, entertainment, and hospitality ticket and booking offices, or the shift of insurance and retail purchases online. Their case admittedly relies on 'yet unforeseen technologies' (p. 135) and so is an extrapolation into the unknown.

In his introduction to the book, Robert Solow questions the effectiveness of retraining proposals, writing that (this) 'certainly does not mean that training the untrained will increase employment' (p. viii), and (that, from the) 'early 1970's the real wage began to fall short of the productivity trend' (p. ix). The labour share of GDP fell from 75 to 67% (p. ix) and by 7% from 2000 (p. 29), falling faster in sectors that use robotics (p. 30). Autor et al. write that 'productivity growth throughout the twentieth century stemmed from technological progress' (p. 126). They argue that the main problem with technology and automation is its unequal impact, because countries other than the US have maintained labour share (p. 4), although other data challenges this claim. Their more detailed arguments for optimism that technology will continue to deliver full employment include that 'history shows technology, full employment, and rising earnings can co-exist' (p. 4), that there is 'no compelling historical or contemporary evidence to suggest that technological advances are driving us towards a jobless future' (p. 7), that 'most of today's jobs hadn't even been invented in 1940' (p. 7), and that 'no rigorous evidence suggests that automation has caused aggregate employment to fall over a sustained time period' (p. 12).

Wage and income distribution is the main issue of concern (p. 16). The US exhibits unique inequality (p. 16). Technology is one common causal factor for this, but other factors explain why the US experience is unique. Over the period 1978–2016, output/hour increased by 66%, but pay for production workers by only 12% (p. 19). Real wages for men with 4 year college degree fell from 1980, to become 10–20% lower by 2017. From 1979 to 2018, the share of GDP going to the US's top income decile rose from 35 to 47% (p. 22), whilst the bottom income quintile's share dropped from 20 to 14%. The causes of this US inequality are (p. 36)

- technological change
- globalisation
- institutional changes.

Between 1979 and 2017, the number of workers in collective bargaining agreements fell from 26 to 12% (p. 37). The US federal real minimum wage in 2020 remained equal to its level in 1950, being 35% less than in 1970 (p. 37).

Their book goes on to analyse the impact of artificial intelligence in the sectors of insurance and health, autonomous vehicles, manufacturing and distribution, and additive manufacturing (p. 41). They claim that outcomes are ambiguous, a question of 'momentous impacts, unfolding gradually' (p. 75). Long gestation timescales apply to the development and implementation of technologies like artificial intelligence. Experience shows a mixture of job displacement and creation. They find that less than 20% of warehouses are automated (p. 59), that the logistics sector has created new jobs (p. 60).

Their policy recommendations are for increased education and training (Chapter 4) which should be specifically defined and focussed by sector and vocation, with online access, and income support. They maintain a work-centric policy perspective, regarding work as superior to social income, specifically, a universal basic income (p. 102). The US federal minimum wage should be increased, (p. 108). Work insurance, health and other benefits, and collective bargaining should be restored. Public sector R&D should increase, because 'the decline in federal research expenditures partly explains the US lacklustre productivity growth rates in the past decade' (p. 125). Capital taxation should be increased to become more in line with labour taxation. In summary, the authors' hope is that 'technological advances are not driving us toward a jobless future' (p. 135), although 'yet unforeseen technologies will not necessarily benefit all workers' (p. 135).

The authors do not consider the environmental implications of their work-led policy recommendations. Since automation inherently implies increased productivity, then a work-led policy will generate yet more output, consumption, resource depletion, and environmental emissions.

This may be one solution to mitigate the prevalent poverty in many developed economies, but all new output would have to be from green technologies if environmental disaster is to be averted. The question which remains 'the elephant in the room' is to what extent poverty is to be addressed by economic growth, and to what extent by radical redistribution.

The challenge then is how to assimilate the above diverse range of findings. An arguable synthesis is that

- The labour share in many economies is reducing.
- Wage inequality within work is increasing.
- These effects are mainly distributional rather than aggregate, and particularly affect lower income quintile groups of the population, whose income is inadequate.
- The effects are at least partially, and some would argue mainly, due to technology and automation.
- Work and wage may therefore not be able to generate adequate income to low-income groups.

Hence the need for radical policy.

Defining Technology and Its Metrics

We have considered how technology might be modelled in an integrated techno-economic paradigm. However, formalising, specifying, and researching such an integrated model of economics and technology requires more exact definitions of technology, and the metrics of technology.

Despite being a major phenomenon not only in economics, but also widely in human experience, technology, as Amartya Sen found with the equally significant concept of justice,[29] proves elusive to define or to measure, which probably accounts for its regrettable absence in standard economic theory.

My own attempt at a definition was 'the cognitive reconfiguration of natural materials and processes',[30] a definition which sought to address the philosophical question of to what extent technology is autonomous and objective, or a result of human agency. It's a definition which unfortunately offers no metrics.

Empirical project research at IPR[31] has tested the hypothesis that technology reduces aggregate disposable income in the economy thus generating a proposal for basic income.

In the project report 'Technological change and growth regimes'[32] the labour share of GDP was used as a surrogate for disposable consumer income. Further work on household income has since tested this assumption.

Various parameters were tested as surrogate measures for technology, i.e.

- the relative price of investment goods to consumption goods
- capital intensity
- capital ratio
- ICT capital ratio
- software capital ratio.

Regressions using four control variables of trade openness, financial integration, union density rate, and age dependency ratio found that only the first variable of the relative price of investment goods demonstrated explanatory power for the decline in labour share. Further refined regressions showed that this overall finding only holds for low-skill employment, and only in certain 'growth regimes'.[33]

Following Popper,[34] this result leads to questioning and re-specification of the hypothesis that technology is responsible for declining aggregate labour income, and its substitution by welfare benefits, pensions, dividends, and household debt.

Specifically we can ask:

- What mechanism explains the effect of the relative price of investment goods on the low-skill labour share in certain growth regimes?
- How can the effect of entirely new investment goods be estimated?
- How can the impact of whole shifts in Kuhnian[35] technology paradigms be estimated?

The latter two questions raise a requirement for a more generic metric of technology. Attempts in the literature to define such a metric have to date proved inconclusive. These are now reviewed.

Metrics of Technology

1 R&D Scoreboards
R&D generates technology, so it offers a potential technology metric. Tracking the effect of R&D on aggregate labour income in a secular study over time in a single economy assumes that its effectiveness and rate of adoption remain equal over that time period. Innovation therefore becomes the more relevant metric. Estimating the same R&D effect in a multi-economy cross-sectional study assumes generic equivalence or ceteris paribus between those economies.

1.1 The EU Innovation Scoreboard (2022)[36] reports innovation performance across countries, both in the EU and globally. This offers a metric of implemented technology which is more relevant to researching the economic impact of technology.

1.2 The Global Innovation Tracker[37] reports short term 1-year growth rates and long-term 10-year growth rates for science and technology publications, R&D, patents, VC deals and value, installed transistors, robots, and labour productivity. R&D expenditure is reported for 2000–2023 in total, by country, sector, and company. The stock of robots is reported to have grown from c700K in 2000 to nearly 3m by 2020.

1.3 OECD/Eurostat's Oslo Manual[38] sets out concepts and definitions for the measurement of innovation. Their team might be able to refer to other organisations which have used this methodology to construct actual metrics of innovation.

2 The Solow Residual
The 'Solow residual' defined by Robert Solow (1957),[39] and refined by others including Edward Denison (1962)[40] attributes growth in economic output not accounted for by growth in labour or capital inputs, as due to technology defined as 'TFP' or total factor

productivity. Solow estimated that 7/8 of growth in labour productivity in the US economy between 1900 and 1949 was due to TFP, i.e. to technology. Nicholas Craft (2008)[41] tracks development in the Solow analysis, showing that capital deepening appears to have a greater effect on labour productivity in S E Asian 'catch-up economies'. Kim and Lim (2004)[42] find that demand variables of exports, money supply, and government spending predict the Solow residual for the South Korean economy, meaning that the Solow residual is over-estimated.

3 Critiques, Discussion, and Development

3.1 Archibugi and Coco (2005)[43] state that 'there is no single number that can provide comprehensive information of the whole technological capabilities of a country, but in spite of these limitations, synthetic indicators can help' (p. 176). They then compare five different metrics of national technological capability developed by WEF, UNDP, UNIDO, RAND, and their own Arco. Each index is a weighted synthesis of components such as patents, R&D, science and technology publications, royalties paid on technology licences, technology infrastructure, trade, human skill sets, and business survey data. They show that the different indices correlate reasonably well, although countries like Israel, Japan, South Korea, Singapore, and Malaysia get ranked differently by each index.

3.2 Lööf, Mairesse, and Mohnen (2016)[44] review the 1998 'CDM' model of Crépon, Duguet, and Mairesse[45] which is a widely used microeconomic firm-level 'structural model that explains productivity by innovation output and the latter by research investment'. Theoretically firm-level results from this model could be aggregated to derive national economy productivity outcomes from R&D/innovation inputs.

3.3 Corrado and Hulten (2010)[46] 'How Do You Measure a "Technological Revolution"?', defined it as 'an increase in the fruits of innovation, as measured by the shift in an aggregate production function (termed multifactor productivity or MFP)' (p. 1). They show that investment in 'intangibles' ('investments in technological expertise, product design, market development, and organizational capability'), has grown consistently over the whole period of 1948–2007, whereas investment in tangibles has only remained constant (p. 6). In the 1995–2017 period, intangibles contributed more to productivity than tangibles (p. 8). Estimates also need to take more account of the impact of product quality on productivity measures (p. 9).

3.4 Radosevic and Yoruk (2016)[47] state that 'technology as one of the major drivers of growth over the long term is not reducible to a single variable such as research and development (R&D) or total factor productivity (TFP)'. They are concerned to develop country-specific metrics for technology which will apply to low- and middle-income countries as well as to high-income countries. They theorise three dimensions for a metric to capture intensity of technology, exploitation, and diversification of technology, and global technology interactions. They critique the GII and EU R&D scoreboards for being atheoretical and merely pragmatic. The CDM model is irrelevant to low-income countries, whilst the WEF metric includes institutional factors which are again a problem for application to low-income countries. The EU scoreboard encourages imitative national technology policy development so that metrics are driving policy rather than policy-driving metrics. They distinguish firm, industry, and national innovation analytics, and claim that low-income countries follow imitative strategies, middle-income countries diversify new technologies, whilst high-income countries operate at the global technology frontier. Their extensive analytical discussion doesn't lead them to propose any actual metrics.

In their further paper (2017),[48] Radosevic and Yoruk state that 'technology upgrading is a multidimensional process and that it would be methodologically wrong to aim for an aggregate index'. Having tested indices of technology intensity, breadth, and exchange, they conclude 'we have given up of constructing an aggregate index of technology upgrading, which would be composed of indexes of intensity and breadth of technology upgrading, and interaction with the global economy'.

Fedyunina and Radosevic (2022)[49] show that imported technology in medium-income countries makes the CDM model linking

R&D to innovation to productivity less relevant. Investment in machinery and equipment proves a better predictor of productivity.

3.5 Eliezer Geisler (1999)[50] provides a long but inconclusive list of factors which could contribute to technology metrics.

3.6 Karabarbounis and Neiman[51] (2013) show the widespread decline in most countries' labour share from 1980 is matched by a decline in the relative price of investment goods. The latter is defined as 'capital rental rates' and so incorporates the interest rate, and explains 50% of the decline in labour share, which generates a large welfare gain. It applies to 42 from 59 countries from 1975 to 2012 with the UK being an exception. The authors conclude that 'investment-specific technology shocks' drive the labour share down. The IPR report referred to above follows Karabarbounis and Neiman's methodology and obtains similar results.

3.7 Abdih and Danninger[52] show the US labour share declining by 3.5% from 2000, after a long period of stability at 56%. They use a metric of the intensity of routinised jobs as a proxy for automation and technology, and find this accounts for 44–57% of the reduction in labour share, with offshoring and increased imports accounting for a further 37–54%, and unionisation a third contributing factor.

Tentative Conclusion

The literature is diverse in its concerns, methodologies, and conclusions, as is fitting to intellectual debate and academic research.

Nevertheless, sufficient evidence emerges of the historic role of technology in reducing labour share. The focus is on the impact of automation in depressing low-quintile incomes, i.e., a distributional more than an aggregate effect. This chimes with the profile of low-quintile income inadequacy and poverty in UK household incomes presented in the Income section of this book. Historic automation to date may be at least partly responsible for low-quintile income inadequacy. The forward concern is that artificial intelligence is displacing higher skill-set labour and represents a serious threat to middle and higher quintile incomes.

If technology is more responsible for income suppression than the political conflict assumed to be inherent to rentier capitalism, then different, more specific, policy solutions are called for. Specifically, high-technology economies may have to accept the inevitability of higher social welfare income as technology limits labour income.

This literature review has focussed on the question of technology's impact on labour income. More comprehensive foundations on techno-economic paradigms are found in the work of Giovanni Dosi,[53] Christopher Freeman,[54] Carlota Perez,[55] and Nathan Rosenberg.[56] Dosi's 2023 'The Foundations of Complex Evolving Economies' shows that technology is the fundamental driver of economic growth. He claims that the market system does not select for firm survival, but that institutional factors predominate. The whole economy is an 'emergent' entity, greater than the sum of its parts, and not reducible to agent rationality. The complex evolving economy is dynamic, requiring a process account. He calls for critical realism in formulating economic theory, and proposes a synthesis of Keynes and Schumpeter to identify 'the feedback between the factors influencing aggregate demand and those driving technological change' (p. 17). Dosi offers a fundamental critique and reformulation of economic theory. His work is significant and important.

Dosi's and others' work tends to stand independently of mainstream economic theory. A synthesis is needed.

References

1. Daron Acemoglu and Pascual Restrepo, *Labor- and Capital-Augmenting Technical Change* (MIT Economics Department Working Paper, 2020).
2. Daron Acemoglu and Pascual Restrepo, *Automation and New Tasks: How Technology Displaces and Reinstates Labor*, Institute of Labor Economics 2019. https://docs.iza.org/dp12293.pdf
3. Rainer Klump, Peter McAdam and Alpo Willman, *Factor Substitution and Factor Augmenting Technical Progress in the US*, 2004, http://www.ecb.europa.eu/pub/pdf/scpwps/ecbwp367.pdf.
4. OECD, *Labour-Saving Technologies and Employment Levels*, 2022, http://www.oecd-ilibrary.org/docserver/9ce86ca5-en.pdf?expires=1688443850&id=id&accname=guest&checksum=D0E2B2B0DE747B7999FD56F38875959E.

5. Katja Mann and Lukas Püttmann, 'Benign Effects of Automation: New Evidence from Patent Texts', *SSRN Electronic Journal*, 2018, https://doi.org/10.2139/ssrn.2959584.
6. D. Autor and D. Dorn, *Automation and Jobs: When Technology Boosts Employment*, 2019, http://www.bu.edu/econ/files/2019/05/JEP_automation_March_29_nber.pdf.
7. Antoine Dechezleprêtre et al., 'Automating Labor: Evidence From Firm-Level Patent Data', *SSRN Electronic Journal*, 2019, https://doi.org/10.2139/ssrn.3508783.
8. D. Acemoglu and P. Restrepo, *Robots and Jobs: Evidence from US Labor Markets*, 2017, https://www.nber.org/system/files/working_papers/w23285/w23285.pdf.
9. Carl Benedikt Frey and Michael A. Osborne, *The Future of Employment: How Susceptible Are Jobs to Computerisation?*, Oxford 2013. https://www.oxfordmartin.ox.ac.uk/publications/the-future-of-employment#:~:text=Carl%20Benedikt%20Frey%20%26%20Michael%20Osborne&text=According%20to%20their%20estimates%2C%20about,an%20occupation's%20probability%20of%20computerisation.
10. Melanie Arntz, Terry Gregory, and Ulrich Zierahn, *The Risk of Automation for Jobs in OECD Countries: A Comparative Analysis* (OECD Publishing, 2016), https://doi.org/10.1787/5jlz9h56dvq7-en.
11. Ljubica Nedelkoska and Glenda Quintini, *Automation, Skills Use and Training* (OECD Publishing, 2018), https://doi.org/10.1787/2e2f4eea-en.
12. Alexandre Georgieff and Agustin Milanez, *What Happened to Jobs at High Risk of Automation?* (OECD Publishing, 2021), https://doi.org/10.1787/10bc97f4-en.
13. Jacopo Staccioli and Maria Enrica Virgillito, 'Back to the Past: The Historical Roots of Labor-Saving Automation', *Eurasian Business Review* 11 (2021): 27–57, https://doi.org/10.1007/s40821-020-00179-1.
14. David Autor and Anna Salomons, *Is Automation Labor-Displacing? Productivity Growth, Employment, and the Labor Share* (Brookings Institution, 2018).
15. Loukas Karabarbounis and Brent Neiman, 'The Global Decline of the Labor Share', *The Quarterly Journal of Economics*

(2014). https://academic.oup.com/qje/article-abstract/129/1/61/1899422
16. William F. Maloney and Carlos Molina, *Is Automation Labor-Displacing in the Developing Countries, Too?*: Robots, Polarization, and Jobs, World Bank Group, 2019, https://ssrn.com/abstract=3438776.
17. Alan Manning, *Explaining Job Polarization: Routine-Biased Technological Change and Offshoring* (London School of Economics Working Paper, 2016).
18. Acemoglu and Restrepo, *Robots and Jobs: Evidence from US Labor Markets*. National Bureau for Economic Research (2017) www.nber.org/papers/w23285
19. J. Doku, *German Robots—The Impact of Industrial Robots on Workers*, 2017, https://doku.iab.de/discussionpapers/2017/dp3017.pdf.
20. ZEW, *Racing With or Against the Machine? Evidence from Europe*, 2016, https://ftp.zew.de/pub/zew-docs/dp/dp16053.pdf.
21. M. Webb, *The Impact of Artificial Intelligence on the Labor Market*, 2020, https://www.michaelwebb.co/webb_ai.pdf.
22. A. Salomons, *Explaining the Labor Share: Automation vs. Labor Market Institutions*, 2022, www.sciencedirect.com/science/article/pii/S0927537122000392.
23. Herbert Dawid and Michael Neugart, Effects of Technological Change and Automation on Industry Structure and (Wage-)Inequality: Insights from a Dynamic Task-Based Model. *Journal of Evolutionary Economics* 33 (2023): 35–63, https://doi.org/10.1007/s00191-022-00803-5.
24. McKinsey, *AI, Automation, and the Future of Work: Ten Things to Solve For*, 2018, www.mckinsey.com/featured-insights/future-of-work/ai-automation-and-the-future-of-work-ten-things-to-solve-for.
25. PricewaterhouseCoopers (PwC), *The International Impact of Automation*, 2018. www.pwc.co.uk/economic-services/assets/international-impact-of-automation-feb-2018.pdf
26. OECD, *The Labour Share in G20 Economies*, 2021, https://www.oecd.org/g20/topics/employment-and-social-policy/The-Labour-Share-in-G20-Economies.pdf.
27. Resolution Foundation, *Dead End Relationship*, 2023. www.resolutionfoundation.org/publications/dead-end-relationship/

28. David Autor, David Mindell, and Elisabeth Reynolds, *The Work of the Future: Building Better Jobs in an Age of Intelligent Machines* (MIT Task Force on the Work of the Future, 2021).
29. Amartya Sen, *The Idea of Justice* (Harvard University Press, 2009).
30. Geoff Crocker, *A Managerial Philosophy of Technology* (Palgrave 2012). www.philosophyoftechnology.com
31. IPR Bath, *The Economics of Basic Income*, https://www.bath.ac.uk/projects/the-economics-of-basic-income/.
32. J. Chrisp, J. Garcia-Lazaro, and O. Pearce, *Technological Change and Growth Regimes*, 2022, www.bath.ac.uk/publications/technological-change-and-growth-regimes/attachments/Technological_growth_regimes_FINAL.pdf.
33. Anke Hassel and Bruno Palier, *Growth and Welfare in Advanced Capitalist Economies* (Oxford University Press, 2021), https://global.oup.com/academic/product/growth-and-welfare-in-advanced-capitalist-economies-9780198866176?cc=us&lang=en&.
34. Karl Popper, *The Logic of Scientific Discovery* (Routledge, 2002).
35. Thomas Kuhn, *The Logic of Scientific Discovery* (University of Chicago Press, 2012), https://press.uchicago.edu/ucp/books/book/chicago/S/bo13179781.html.
36. *The EU Innovation Scoreboard 2022*, 2022, https://ec.europa.eu/.
37. *Global Innovation Tracker*, 2023, https://globalinnovationtracker.com.
38. Organisation for Economic Co-operation and Development (OECD), *Oslo Manual 2018: Guidelines for Collecting, Reporting, and Using Data on Innovation*, 2018.
39. Robert M. Solow, *Technical Change and the Aggregate Production Function*, The Review of Economics and Statistics, 1957.
40. Edward F. Denison, *The Sources of Economic Growth in the United States and the Alternatives Before Us* (Committee for Economic Development, 1962).
41. Nicholas Craft, 'Development in the Solow Analysis', *Journal of Economic Perspectives*, 2008.
42. Soojung Kim and Gi-won Lim, 'Predicting the Solow Residual for South Korea's Economy', *Economic Analysis*, 2004.
43. Daniele Archibugi and Alberto Coco, 'Measuring Technological Capabilities at the Country Level: A Survey and a Critical Analysis', *Research Policy* 34, no. 2 (2005): 175–194.

44. Hans Lööf, Jacques Mairesse, and Pierre Mohnen, 'Review of the CDM Model of Crépon, Duguet and Mairesse', *Research Policy*, 2016.
45. Bruno Crépon, Emmanuel Duguet, and Jacques Mairesse, 'Research, Innovation and Productivity: An Econometric Analysis at the Firm Level', *Economics of Innovation and New Technology* 7, no. 2 (1998): 115–58, https://doi.org/10.1080/10438599800000031.
46. Carol Corrado and Charles Hulten, 'How Do You Measure a "Technological Revolution"?', *Research Policy*, 2010.
47. Slavo Radosevic and Esin Yoruk, 'Country Specific Metrics for Technology Growth', *Research Policy*, 2016.
48. Slavo Radosevic and Ece Yoruk, *'Technology Upgrading of Middle-Income Economies: A New Approach and Results'* (Elsevier, 2017).
49. Anastasia Fedyunina and Slavo Radosevic, 'Imported Technology in Medium-Income Countries and Productivity', *Economics of Innovation and New Technology*, 2022.
50. Eliezer Geisler, *Metrics of Science and Technology: Evaluating R&D and Innovation* (Quorum Books, 1999).
51. Karabarbounis and Neiman, 'The Global Decline of the Labor Share'. *The Quarterly Journal of Economics* (2013) https://academic.oup.com/qje/article-abstract/129/1/61/1899422
52. Yasser Abdih and Stephan Danninger, *The Declining Labor Share in the United States*, IMF Working Paper, 2017. www.imf.org/en/Publications/WP/Issues/2017/07/24/What-Explains-the-Decline-of-the-U-S-45086
53. Giovanni Dosi, *The Foundations of Complex Evolving Economies: Part One: Innovation, Organization, and Industrial Dynamics* (Oxford University Press, 2023).
54. Christopher Freeman and Luc Soete, *Technical Change And Full Employment* (Blackwell, 1987).
55. Wolfgang Drechsler, Erik Reinert, and Rainer Kattel, *Techno-Economic Paradigms: Essays in Honour of Carlota Perez* (Anthem Press, 2009).
56. Nathan Rosenberg, *Technology and the Wealth of Nations* (Stanford University Press, 1992).

On Policy

Abstract A Summary of policy proposals.

Keyword Policy

This section is deliberately brief in order to offer succinct policy proposals. The above **analysis** has argued

- the inadequacy of individual and household income for substantial population groups
- the fundamental ontology of money as created, not as debt
- the role of technological automation in reducing the labour share of GDP and low-quintile income
- the likely extension of this income reduction effect to middle-income groups.

The set of **radical policy proposals** emerging from this analysis are

- accept
    - a reduced role for work and wage in providing income
    - a necessarily increased role for social welfare income

- introduce a hybrid social income scheme to deliver adequate individual and household income, with
    - a low universal income floor
    - targeted benefits with substantially reduced conditionality
- reverse the increase in pension age
- formally permit direct money financing of government expenditure
- retire government debt over time by central bank purchase by direct money financing
- deploy high productivity technology widely
- incentivise green technology.

On Theory—An Appendix

Abstract This chapter provides a critical review of mainstream economic theory, challenging the adequacy of price as the primary determinant of demand and supply. It critiques neoclassical models for their reliance on simplified assumptions about consumer and firm behaviour, arguing that real economic processes are far more complex, involving psychological, social, and random factors. The chapter advocates for a more realistic approach to economic theory, incorporating technology, income, and the dynamics of supply and demand. It also explores the limitations of mathematical models in economics and calls for an integration of empirical and theoretical approaches to better understand economic outcomes.

Keywords Economic theory · Price elasticity · Consumer demand · Supply and demand curve · Mathematical models · Neoclassical economics · Keynes · Keynesian economics · Monetarism · Behavioural economics · Rational agents · Marginal utility

Defining Economics

Economics seeks to understand the economy, that is, the processes by which resources are turned into goods and services. Economics is both *theory* and *policy*. As *theory* it seeks to explain the economy as an observed phenomenon. It forms speculative intellectual paradigms and hypotheses of how the economy works. It builds models to enable *predictions* and *simulations* of economic outcomes.

As an intellectual process economics purports to be objective. But in reality, it reflects or even advocates a political concept. The role of government, the role of the market, the interaction of labour and capital, the distribution of income and wealth, the environmental impact of resource exploitation and emissions are all an inevitable part of economic theorising, and render economics inevitably political.

Economics as *policy* is consciously political. Economic policy pursues selected objectives. These may include economic growth, elimination of poverty, best ecological outcomes, consumer lifestyle and standard of living, civic, community, and cultural goals and aspirations, education and health outcomes, and social justice. The choice and prioritisation of these objectives are political and social.

Economics as Theory

A frequent starting point for economic thinking is the joint claim of scarcity of resources with insatiability of demand. This tension requires selective allocation. In a 'command economy', allocation is achieved by fiat. In a market economy, itself therefore a political option, allocation is claimed to be achieved by price. Price becomes the dominant concept in market economics, with a pervasive hegemony. Marxist economics sees power as the fundamental variable determining price.

Price is preeminent at every introduction to market economics. Students learn that consumer demand for products and services depends on their price, typically reducing with price to form the famous downward sloping demand curve of quantity vs price. At the same time, price determines supply, in this case supply increasing with price to generate the equally famous upward sloping demand curve, which is a highly questionable claim as most producers face economies of scale and declining marginal cost. These two curves intersect at a point defining the quantity of the product or service supplied and consumed in the market, and its price. This simple mini-model is ubiquitous in economics textbooks and in general economics thinking. It appears elegant, has some intellectual appeal, claims to 'solve' markets, and offers thought simulations, for example what happens to the price/quantity outcome as consumer income shifts the demand curve, or enhanced production technology shifts the supply curve. Moreover it sets a precedent for a wide range of further economic theorising, hypotheses, and models of increasing mathematical complexity and splendour.

But there are reasons to question whether this approach to economic thinking is delusional. The supply/demand curve model faces the challenge that it is a meaningless tautology, rather than an explanation. This becomes evident when the shape of the demand curve for any product or service is considered. The general claim is that the curve is 'downward sloping', i.e. that a lower price generates increased demand and a higher price reduces demand. But how downward sloping is each product demand curve? This pushes the model's proponents to the concept of 'elasticity' of demand. So the extent to which price determines demand now depends on the price *elasticity* of demand, which can apparently range from totally inelastic, where price has no effect on demand at all rendered by a vertical demand curve, to totally elastic where price is constant for all quantities demanded, to negative where increased price leads to increased demand in the famous case of so-called Giffin goods. At this point, the sceptic might be forgiven for concluding that the basic model is inadequate, and that price fails to uniquely explain demand. Defenders of the model seek to circumnavigate these difficulties by allowing the demand curve to 'shift' position, for example, to shift rightwards in response to increased consumer income. What should be admitted is that introducing the concept of price elasticity of demand shifts the burden of explanation of demand from price itself to a need to explain price elasticity. And yet no such explanation of price elasticity is offered. The model is limited to a two-dimensional visual representation and therefore can only include two explanatory variables for demand, one being price along the curve, and the second being income by shifting the curve. Limiting an explanation of demand to only two variables is clearly inadequate as economic theory.

In reality, price affects demand, but only to some extent. It does not uniquely determine demand. Let's look at some real-life examples. Television interviewers love to mock politicians, including UK Prime Ministers, for not knowing 'the price of a pint (0.568 litre!) of milk', claiming that such ignorance proves that politicians are out of touch. Many of us would have to admit also to not knowing this price. In fact, the answer is quite complex. It depends on where the milk is bought, whether full cream, skimmed, or semi-skimmed milk is bought, and how much is bought. In a British supermarket in early 2024, one pint of milk costs 90p, 2 pints cost £1.20, i.e. 60p/pint and 4 pints costs £2.15, i.e. 53.75p/pint. Milk delivered to the doorstep might cost £1.15/pint or £1.45/pint for its organic variant. So what is the price of a pint of milk? The answer lies between 53.75p and £1.45, a difference of 2.7 times! Lest any enthusiast thinks this is data for a demand curve for milk, I'll point out that it's not, because the product is different and not homogenous at each price point. Delivered milk, bulk milk, and organic milk are related but heterogeneous products. Indeed the bulk milk product depends on the consumer having refrigeration capacity, so that the received price of milk depends on the cost of a cubic litre of refrigerator space! How does a demand curve address that? And how does consumer demand respond to this price set? We can imagine that if substantial price hikes occurred, then consumers might seek lower price options, but most consumers may well not be able or willing to adjust to minor price changes. Similar problems arise when considering the price of telephone calls. Take a system where subscribers pay per minute. Callers may exercise restraint when making calls known to be expensive, for example international calls, or system accesses requiring large data downloads. But many callers may be unaware of the cost of a current phone call they are making, only seeing its effect later in their monthly bill. Is it likely however that if the relative price of milk compared to the price of telephone calls changed, that consumers would switch demand from milk to telephone calls, or vice versa? Given the plethora of products and services consumed in today's market economies, it would surely be impossible for any consumer to adjust their purchases to maximise their utility according to fluctuations in the set of relative prices? Yet this is precisely what standard economic theory claims.

A further challenge to the price theory of demand is that products and services are rarely identical. In fact, suppliers actively seek to differentiate their product or service to diminish the relative importance of simple price in determining its demand. Product specifications vary widely and evolve constantly. After-sales service is emphasised as a competitive advantage. Free delivery may be offered, along with various loyalty schemes to retain existing customers. Any experienced business manager will know that location-specific price/performance determines demand, rather than price alone. Advertising expenditure, creation of brand awareness, etc. are all potentially far more determining of demand than price. Whilst business-to-business demand may be capable of more careful calculation in its purchasing function, consumer demand is more psychological and determined by income constraints biting against cumulative expenditures, rather than by price alone acting directly.

And yet the obsession with price continues unabated into almost all domains of 'mainstream' market economic theory. In neoclassical economics, wage was regarded as the price of labour. According to this view, employment would therefore be increased by a reduction in wages. This conceptual error, unequivocally corrected by Keynes, led to huge failures in economic management and to widespread social misery. Even Keynes however suggested that labour would be supplied to the point at which the wage rate equalled 'the marginal disutility of labour', which is also a tautology rather than an explanation.

Equally, contemporary monetary theory regards the interest rate as the price of money, and attempts to manage the total macroeconomy through this single instrument. In particular, conventional wisdom is that nominally independent central banks have to set the interest rate to manage inflation. This is despite the fact that the interest rate has multiple effects on the economy, some of which are actually counter-productive to the management of inflation. In an economy where many people own houses funded by a mortgage, an interest rate increase will reduce their disposable income. This might reduce their demand, and hence reduce inflationary pressure in the economy, but even this is not necessarily so. Consumers might alternatively maintain demand by reducing saving, drawing on existing savings, taking out loans, or increasing their working hours. Since many consumers hold fixed rate mortgages, there will be a substantial lag in consumer demand to an interest rate change.

For businesses with loans, the interest rate increase will increase costs which may well be passed on in prices, actually increasing inflation. Higher interest rates may deter investment, thereby restricting supply, also likely to be inflationary. Since the interest rate is likely to have contradictory effects on consumer disposable income, and business operating costs and investment decisions, there may be a valid argument for applying differential interest rates to the consumer sector of the economy compared to the business sector, rather than operating one homogenous interest rate across the whole economy. If defining different interest rates proves impractical because of the homogeneity of money, then the same effect might be achieved by the application of interest payment taxes in each sector? A further factor is that hot money will be attracted to buy a currency with a higher interest rate, thus tending to increase its exchange rate, which will mitigate inflation via the effect on imported goods and services, but at the same time, worsen the balance of trade, reducing exports and employment in exporting sectors.

The parallel obsession with demand/supply market analysis insists on regarding inflation as a result of excess demand over supply, or 'too much money chasing too few goods'. It's curious that the policy response even to this limited diagnostic is always to seek to reduce demand via quasi consumer tax increases and business cost increases generated by increasing the interest rate. Logically, if excess demand is thought to be the cause of inflation, then an equally effective policy would be to seek to increase supply. Inflation could be addressed by economic growth rather than by economic decline. In the long run, it is the pervasive deployment of high technology production which has consistently and inexorably reduced real prices, hence increasing the standard of living. In cases of imported inflation, e.g. the 1970s OPEC oil price hike, or the 2020s global supply side price hikes resulting from the war in Ukraine and Covid shutdowns in China, efficient export growth would also offer a better response. But inflation may have other causes, classically a political cause in the struggle for shares in economic output. Workers may simply demand wage increases, or resource-rich states impose price increases. These are distributional rather than allocative or technological causes of inflation. Orthodox inflation correction policy of increasing the interest rate may then have no effect at all. There is clearly a need for greater nuance in formulating inflation correction policy.

Neoclassical theory also regarded the interest rate as the cost of capital investment and the price of savings, and claimed that a downward sloping investment curve would intersect an upward sloping savings curve to determine and equalise the amounts of investment and saving, whilst also determining the interest rate which equated them. This despite the obvious Keynesian reality that it is future consumption which prompts investment, not current or future saving. This discussion at least shows the inadequacy of a simple price theory applied to money as its interest rate to manage the economy. We got there because monetary theory tried to manage the economy via the quantity of money. But this proved impossible, as money creation by commercial banks making loans to businesses and individuals, as well as individuals expanding money in use via their credit cards, became uncontrollable. Hence monetarism resorted to the price of money, the interest rate, as its simple single instrument.

Similar delusions apply to supply in the economy. The standard claim is that firms produce to a point where marginal cost equals marginal revenue. This stunning simplicity is derived from elementary calculus. Since

$$Profit = Revenue - Cost$$

then if we assume that all three variables are quantity (Q) related, then we can differentiate this equation to show that

$$\frac{d(Profit)}{dQ} = \frac{d(Revenue)}{dQ} - \frac{d(Cost)}{dQ}$$

Setting

$$\frac{d(Profit)}{dQ} = 0$$

which is the requirement for maximisation in the theory of calculus, gives us that, for profit maximisation, marginal revenue must equal marginal cost. This is typical of the procedures for building more complex mathematical models in both microeconomics and macroeconomics. They are intellectually appealing as abstractions, and offer apparent mathematical solutions and simulations. Standard professional economics journals abound with such mathematical expositions, making them inaccessible to the general reader, and therefore beyond challenge. They fail the Popperian test of being falsifiable because they are not even comprehensible.

A review of two leading economics textbooks widely used for university students' introductory courses demonstrates the extent to which abstract mathematical models and price theory currently dominate economic theory.

1. **Hal Varian's 'Intermediate Microeconomics'**[1] is set as the introductory reader to the undergraduate economics course at Cambridge University, UK. Varian presents a plethora of elegant mathematical formulae, models, and tools, from bi-product consumer indifference curves matched against budget constraints, to producer profit maximisation, marginal factor productivity, isoquants et al. None of these either describe or explain real-world consumers and firms. They neither derive from, nor refer to, the real economy. Instead, Varian offers a mythical world of marginalist mathematical economics which generates toy models with no relevance to economic theory or policy. His approach is entirely theory led. Karl Popper's scientific methodology was to observe phenomena, propose explanatory hypotheses, and test their implications empirically. Alternatively, Thomas Kuhn offered a theory of paradigm change. Varian follows neither of these methodologies, disqualifying his presentation of economics as science. Real microeconomics addresses the behaviour of consumers and producers in real markets in real industry sectors. Mathematical modelling is a useful tool in such theorising and research, but not as an end in itself, which is what it sadly has become in current academic mainstream microeconomics exemplified by Varian's book.

2. **Charles Jones 'Macroeconomics'**[2] is the equivalent introduction to macroeconomics set in the same Cambridge UK undergraduate course introduction. Although impressive in its coverage and detail, Jones's book exemplifies the inadequacies and errors in contemporary economic theory. Jones uncritically propounds the neoclassical view in which the economy is a finely tuned instrument responding and adjusting to price signals. From this he builds an elaborate elegant mathematical model which can then be 'solved' to determine the economy, simulate responses, and inform policy. The problem is that the mathematical model is a myth, failing to represent how the real economy actually works. Although Keynes gets 3 fleeting references (compared to 13 for Friedman), there is zero mention in Jones's book of the Keynesian revolution, in which the

economy is a plumbing system which can get stuck in blockages, instead of the neoclassical finely tuned instrument which always adjusts to equilibrium. According to Jones, the labour market adjusts its supply and demand according to its price, i.e. the wage, against the marginal productivity of labour. Investment responds to its price, i.e. the interest rate, against the marginal productivity of capital, and is led and funded by savings. Like the supply and demand model set out earlier, Jones's account of the economy is a tautology which explains nothing.

As Keynes so convincingly pointed out, wage is not only the price of labour, but also the enabler of effective demand, which boosts expected consumption, which is the real determinant of business investment, rather than either the interest rate or savings. Increased wages can therefore increase, rather than decrease, employment.

On monetary theory, Jones claims that central banks create money, whereas central banks themselves explain that it's commercial banks which create money for business and individual loans, and earn its seigniorage. Central banks are in fact explicitly proscribed from direct money creation to fund government expenditure, a proscription they commonly overcome by (scandalously) purchasing their own government's debt in secondary markets. He wrongly assumes that money is necessarily debt at the point of its creation, and thus follows the error of orthodox accountancy, masquerading as economics, in viewing debt/GDP ratios as a real constraint. He makes no mention and therefore offers no critique, of modern monetary theory. He claims that the labour share of GDP is constant, whereas in fact, it's declining. He therefore misses important arguments for an increased proportion of non-labour income, whether as pensions, welfare benefits, dividends, or household debt. He makes no mention of huge dysfunctionalities in contemporary economies, ranging from gross inequality, through in-work poverty, low wage, bullshit jobs, austerity, and ecological damage. His macroeconomics is disengaged theory. His belief in the efficacy of the interest rate

> to control the economy and the Taylor rule to control inflation is delusional.
>
> Most importantly, Jones fails to include technology in his economic theory. Both in its constant creation of new and better products and services, and in its equally constant evolution of production functions to higher levels of productivity, it is technology working through effective industrial management which determines and transforms economies. Jones is not alone in this omission—it is a core failure of mainstream economics.

This summary critique of Jones and similar university undergraduate textbooks presages a review of economics as policy, which then leads to an attempt to reformulate both theory and policy.

The critique of all such economic theory from the perspective of philosophical realism is that the real economy simply does not work in the way mainstream theory assumes. Consumers do not maximise utility by purchasing according to product indifference curves they carry around in their heads (see Levin and Milgrom's 2004 Stanford paper 'Consumer Theory'[3] for example. The microeconomics course at MIT[4] is similar). Firms are simply unable to operate with advance capability and information to maximise profit, or to produce to a point where marginal revenue equals marginal cost. Empirical work with consumers and firms can readily verify this to be the case. Mainstream conceptual theorists, who rarely visit either a consumer or a firm, then seek to defend their theoretical methodology by claiming that, even if the real economy does not operate as they assume, it can be said to behave 'as if' their assumptions were true. This 'as if' conceptualisation is the only refuge available to mainstream thinking. But does it have even a shred of validity? Milton Friedman attempted to justify this 'as if' methodology in his 1966 paper 'The Methodology of Positive Economics'.[5] Friedman's claim that science operates according to whether its theories have predictive power rather than whether its assumptions are true, and that professional billiard players expertise can be understood 'as if' they were solving complex mathematical vectors, is ably dismissed by George Blackford in his 2017 paper 'On the Pseudo-Scientific Nature of Friedman's as if Methodology'.[6] The realism and truth of assumptions do matter to the validity of any theoretical hypothesis. Particle physics may be able to justify its research by hypothesising the existence of particles and testing empirically to see whether phenomena behave 'as if' these hypothesised particles exist. But this tentative research methodology into the unknown does not extend to situations where an assumption is known to be untrue. The demonstrable falsity of the behavioural assumptions of mainstream economics' consumer theory and its theory of the firm invalidates the elegant complex mathematical structures built on these assumptions. The whole edifice of the Chicago marginal school of economic theory collapses. The collapse is not only evident in rational intellectual challenge, but also empirically in its failure to diagnose the contemporary global economy meaningfully, and in the failure of its consequent policies which have led to extensive economic dysfunctionality with grave social and environmental consequences.

The Significance of Price

This doesn't at all mean that price is insignificant. In fact price has a wider and deeper significance than mainstream price theory allows. Price is a complex indicator which reports three very significant measures, those of allocation, efficiency, and distribution. The relative price of any product or service signals the consumer appeal of the product compared to others products. Whilst consumer choice and behaviour depend on a far wider range of variables than price alone, price remains one important determinant of consumer choice. This is the allocative aspect of price. Price also signals the technological efficiency of production of the product or service. In a market economy, price must at least cover the cost of production and delivery of the product. More efficient production, typically by automation and its economies of scale, will reduce the cost of the product and therefore could reduce its price. Whether it will reduce its price depends on market conditions for the product, and the competitive strategy of its supplier. Nevertheless, price, like wage, signals potential opportunity for technological innovation to optimise production and delivery costs. But price also incorporates distributive information. Price determines the share of product value as it is distributed between the consumer and the producer. A high price distributes profit to the producer, which may then further be distributed between labour and capital. A low price distributes surplus to consumers. Here, the downward sloping demand curve does have some analytical value. Most market prices are homogenous, i.e. the same for all consumers. Some consumers however would have been willing to pay a higher price, and so benefit from the prevailing market price. These consumers form the section of the downward sloping demand curve to the left of its intersection with the supply curve. The area of the demand/supply curve diagram between the demand curve to the left of its intersection with the supply curve, and the determined market price, represents the aggregate consumer surplus generated. Firms often seek to reduce this consumer surplus through the practice of discriminatory pricing, extracting a higher price from consumers willing to pay more. A regular example is in transport. Airlines, rail, and bus companies set higher prices for specific consumer groups by applying price conditions calibrated for each group. Business travel, which is often a short-term decision, attracts a higher price than tourist travel which tends to be decided more in advance by average lower income consumer groups. Business and first class travel sets prices which are very much higher than the additional supply costs required, essentially increasing the net consumer price.

Mainstream economics price theory, whilst making price core to its analysis, nevertheless ignores these two other aspects of price, i.e. those of technical efficiency and of social distribution. This again highlights and exemplifies the need to extend economic theory to include technology, and to include social analysis.

Economics as Mathematics

Mathematics is an abstraction, a language, and a subset of deductive logic. It therefore does have powerful potential in application to economics. Insisting on realism in economic theory does not exclude the use of mathematics in economics. The philosophy of mathematics debates whether maths is discovered or invented. Stewart Shapiro makes a good case for the objectivity of mathematics by pointing out that an infinite number of prime numbers exists, but we cannot know them, meaning that they are discovered and not invented.[7] Realism still relies on abstraction. Every written word, every counted quantity, every arithmetic process, is an abstraction. Mathematics is therefore acceptable as a contributing abstraction to economic thought. The crucial requirement is that any mathematical, or even simple arithmetic process, must refer, i.e. derive from and conclude into the matching real-world phenomena. To give a simple example, negative numbers do not refer, as there is no real-world existence of a negative quantity. Nevertheless, a negative number can be used in calculation, or in an equation, as long as the end result of the calculation does correspond correctly to a real-world phenomenon.

The objection however is that mathematics too readily displaces economic thought. We end up with extremely complex mathematical models based on extremely simplistic and even invalid assumptions. Mathematics has become an end in itself, the end rather than the means. Keynes first read mathematics at Cambridge before turning to economics, and so was mathematically competent. Nevertheless, he was scathing of the displacement of economic thought by mathematical modelling, writing in his 1936 General Theory, 'too large a proportion of recent "mathematical" economics are mere concoctions, as imprecise as the initial assumptions they rest on, which allow the author to lose sight of the complexities and interdependencies of the real world in a maze of pretentious and unhelpful symbols' (p. 298), concluding 'I do not myself attach much value to manipulations of this kind....I doubt if they carry us any further than ordinary discourse can' (p. 305).

More realistic assumptions about consumer and firm behaviour likely prove to be more complex, suggesting that the mathematics required to model them would be mega-complex or beyond the current capability of maths itself. It's notable that this surge or takeover of mathematics has developed in tandem with the marginal school in economics. Differential calculus, discovered by Newton and Leibniz, is intellectually elegant and appealing. Quadratic and higher power functions can be differentiated, their differential set equal to zero to identify maximum and minimum points, depending on the sign of the second differential. The potential application to an economic theory based on consumers maximising utility and firms maximising profit is evident. But if the world simply doesn't work that way, then complex modelling is misguided. In comparison, maximisation of linear functions defied solution by calculus since a linear function cannot be differentiated. It took the pioneering work of the Russian mathematician Leonid Kantorovich,[8] winner together with Tjalling Koopmans of the 1975 Nobel Prize in economics,[9] whose work was later developed by George Dantzig into the Simplex algorithm,[10] to solve linear programmes. Linear programming works by an iterative process to reach the maximum or minimum solution by identifying the 'shadow price' of pivotal variables whose values are then changed. Iterative action by consumers and firms until budget constraints are met appears closer to linear programming methodology than to the smooth optimisation of marginal economics and differential calculus.

Language is a tool of communication. Mathematics as language faces the challenge of fluency, the extent of proficiency in the language. If only a small community is proficient in the language, then it faces severe limits to its ability to communicate, and extreme limits to any challenge to the ideas it seeks to propagate. It is doubtful that a wide community can become fluent in the level of mathematics widely used in economics papers. Economics should therefore ensure that, when it uses complex mathematics, it also offers a translation into a more widely used language such as English to communicate its ideas and to enable challenge and debate.

Gottlob Frege defined mathematics as logic.[11] In this role, mathematics has much to offer economics as a discipline to check and verify its ideas. This is particularly true if mathematics is considered to be discovered rather than invented, i.e. to be objective. Representing consumption functions, investment functions, government expenditure, tax rates, imports, etc. mathematically within an overall simulation model is an important contribution to economics, both to test theory, and to develop policy. This process makes economics empirical and thus real. So the objection is not against representing a consumption function mathematically. The requirement is that the function should be based on real assumptions of consumer behaviour. The use of regression models to test economic hypotheses, or to research causal relationships between economic variables, is also valid and important. In some ways though, it has become economics itself, to the loss of any focus on underlying economic philosophy.

Economics as Policy

Economic policy seeks to achieve objectives which are determined socially and politically.

These objectives typically include sustainable economic growth, price stability, full employment, high productivity, 'sound' public finance, relative equality, adequate consumer income, good health, education, and lifestyle outcomes.

Instead the combination of the raw economy coupled with economic policy has delivered substantial economic and social dysfunctionality. Recent and current experience includes a global economic crisis, pervasive household and government debt, continuous austerity policy, extensive poverty, specifically including in-work poverty, rampant inequality, and environmental damage threatening climate catastrophe.

This has to rate as a failure of economic policy. To the extent that economic theory informs economic policy, it strongly suggests a failure of economic theory too. A rethink is needed, but as is ever the case, orthodoxy resists any such rethink.

Whilst there are many aspects of economic theory which might be considered for such a rethink, the three issues which are the focus of this book are those of income, money, and technology. The pressing reason for this focus is the obvious and urgent need to deliver income adequacy to people, and to get debt out of the economic system, both at household and government level. The focus on technology is due to the fundamental importance of technology to the economy and its outcomes, an importance which has been comprehensively ignored in mainstream economic theory.

Keynes and the Fundamental Nature of the Economy

Contemporary heterodox economics frequently calls for theory which addresses the question of how the economy really works in practice, rather than building elaborate mathematical edifices on the basis of simplistic assumptions.

Keynes published his *'General Theory of Employment, Interest and Money'* in 1936 to address the 1930s global economic depression. He made numerous innovations, challenging the dominant paradigm of neoclassical economics. He fundamentally criticised price theory, whether price as labour's wage, or price as capital's interest rate, in both cases showing that a reduction in their 'price' may well not be effective in increasing the demand for labour or capital respectively. Neoclassical economists argued that the answer to unemployment was for workers to 'price themselves into work' by lowering wages. This, they claimed, would increase demand for labour, reduce production cost thus stimulating demand, and lead to full employment. Keynes developed an alternative theory of wages, in which the wage is not only a cost of production, but also funds effective demand. Lower wages might reduce the cost of production as the neo-classicists expected, but they would also reduce demand, and therefore employment which relies on demand.

Keynes also developed the concept of the multiplier, by which an initial demand stimulus, such as a government investment project, would have a multiplied effect, as wage earners then spent their earned income. Keynes showed arithmetically that the multiplier is equal to the inverse of the marginal propensity to save. He also challenged the neoclassical view that investment depends on savings, correctly claiming the opposite, i.e. that it is consumption, and more importantly, expected future consumption, which is the main incentive to invest. Businesses invest to sell future products and services, and therefore need to have confidence of future aggregate demand. This is a longer-term additional multiplier effect of an initial fiscal stimulus to the economy. In his theory of liquidity preference, Keynes also argued that neither does the interest rate necessarily determine investment. Low interest rates which are often thought to stimulate investment by reducing its cost, can in fact persuade people to hoard cash rather than invest, if higher future interest rates are expected. Investment might therefore also not respond to an increase in the money supply.

For Keynes, government budgets do not always have to be balanced, as deficit funded spending can raise employment and output to generate an expanded tax base and future government revenue surplus. Policies of demand management resulted from Keynesian economic theory, implemented for example in Roosevelt's 'New Deal'. Despite a latter-day tendency to disregard Keynes, Keynesian demand management has become an established part of all governments' macroeconomic policy ever since.

Keynes did not however reject the marginalist paradigm in its entirety. In summarising his 'general theory' in Chapter 18 of his book, he states his independent variables to be the marginal propensity to consume, the marginal efficiency of capital, and the interest rate (p. 245). His dependent variables are aggregate employment and output (GDP). He takes as given the quantity and skill set of labour, the existing productive capital stock, competitive market positioning, consumer tastes, and most importantly, technology. His theory of investment is that investment will increase to the point where the 'marginal efficiency of capital' equals the interest rate. His theory of the labour market is that labour supply will increase to the point where the 'marginal disutility of labour' equals the wage rate. He is orthodox on the question of money creation, regarding money as debt, with government debt needing to be repaid, but in the long term, allowing for temporary government deficits.

By taking so many economic variables as fixed and given, Keynes's theory is only 'general' in a very specific sense, i.e. that of showing that the system could and did converge to an equilibrium position of less than full employment. His theory of wage as demand and not only cost was revolutionary, as was his insistence that investment depended on expected demand, not on current savings. Even his allowance of temporary government deficit spending as a stimulus to the economy was creative.

A truly general economic theory would have to allow the variables of labour, capital, and particularly technology to vary. The key importance of technology in economic theory has continued to be neglected.

> A key reformulation of economic thinking in Keynes is a revolution in the view of how the real economy works.
> In the neoclassical view, a market economy is a finely tuned mechanism, which responds sensitively, exactly, and fully to price signals so as to clear markets to equilibrium, and specifically to full employment.
> In Keynesian economics, the market economy is seen to be more like a plumbing system which can get blocked, than a finely tuned mechanism which always responds to regain perfect equilibrium. There can be blockages in the economic system.
> I am grateful to the late Richard (Dick) Morley, former head of department of economics at Durham university UK, for this metaphor.

Axel Leijonhufvud in his 1968 *'On Keynesian Economics and the Economics of Keynes'*,[12] pointed out that information can fail to flow between actors in the economy, so that unfulfilled demand or supply can block the system, leading to involuntary unemployment.

This change in metaphor is crucial to economic thinking. In considering real economy consumer, production, labour, and investment functions, it will become evident that a wide range of determinants other than price affect economic behaviour. Outcomes are random as much as they result from consumer or producer rationality.

This section concludes with a brief summary of Keynes's General Theory by chapter, and some choice quotes.

John Maynard Keynes The General Theory of Employment, Interest, and Money

MacMillan 1936

A summary by chapter

Chapter	Summary
1	Classical theory is a special case and not reality Pigou's 'Theory of Unemployment' is the special case, Keynes's theory the general case
2	Classical theory equates wage to the marginal output of labour Keynes says unemployment is of 3 types, frictional, voluntary, and involuntary Labour supply is a function of the money wage, not the real wage, since labour supply is not sensitive to inflation and does not calculate the real wage 'There has been a fundamental misunderstanding of how in this respect the economy in which we live actually works' (p. 13) Keynes defines involuntary unemployment where inflation creates labour demand and supply in excess of actual employment (p. 15) But Keynes still says that employment will increase if the real wage decreases, because of decreasing return to production Say's Law incorrectly claims that supply creates its own demand, and that savings create investment
3	Investment is a function of the marginal efficiency of capital Employment is a function of aggregate demand (p. 29)—this is the 'essence of the General Theory' If employment increases and the marginal propensity to consume is less than 1, then consumption will not increase sufficiently, requiring investment, which if lacking, creates unemployment Consumption plus investment create employment and determine the wage (p. 30) Keynes still postulates the 'marginal disutility of labour' Insufficiency of effective demand is key (p. 31) A rich society consumes less, so needs higher investment But Keynes is curiously very critical of C H Douglas's under-consumption theory (pp. 32, 371)
4	On units, expectations, and income Measurement of output, productivity, and technology suffer from 'mock precision' (p. 40)

(continued)

ON THEORY—AN APPENDIX

(continued)

Chapter	Summary
5	Output is a function of expectations, plus fluctuations, oscillations, and feed-back loops
6	Definitions of income, savings and investment
	Employment is a function of firms' profit maximisation (p. 55)
	Long section on business accounting and depreciation
	Investment = saving = income minus consumption, but are these a priori or ex-post?
7	On savings and investment
8	What determines employment? (p. 89) The aggregate demand function (p. 89)
	Employment is a function of consumption and investment
	Consumption is a function of the interest rate, especially if mortgages are dominant
	Consumption is a function of wage (p. 96)
	Consumption is a function of income
	If income increases, savings increase, because consumption is 'habitual' (p. 97)
	Depreciation reduces income and therefore reduces consumption (p. 100)
	A reduction in the marginal propensity to consume reduces demand for consumption and investment
9	Keynes sets out 8 incentives to save and 6 incentives to consume (p. 108)
	If the interest rate increases, savings will decrease, investment, income and consumption will decrease so savings will then also decrease
	An increase in the interest rate only increases savings if income is unchanged
	On the interest rate, Keynes mocks 'the tribute that classical economics pays to her' (p. 112)
10	Reviews R F Kahn's 1931 multiplier
	Mocks monetary policy solutions proposing to bury bottles containing banknotes to be dug up (p. 129), but building housing is a better policy
11	On investment. The marginal efficiency of capital equals the expected NPV, determines capital
12	Investment is a process of trial and error, led by 'animal spirits'
13	On the interest rate
14	In classical theory the interest rate is a price equating investment and savings, like demand and supply
15	On cash, and detail of bond market practice
16	Saving reduces investment
17	Compares money to other assets. Proposes a carrying cost (p. 234)
	An increased interest rate reduces output because the money supply is fixed and can't be increased
	'Inelasticity of supply of money because of the gold standard is the problem' (p. 236)

(continued)

(continued)

Chapter	Summary
	Liquidity preference exceeds the cost of carrying money Money is like land, with inelasticity of supply An increase in the interest rate will increase liquidity preference to hold money Poverty is due to 'liquidity preference' for land and money (p. 242)
18	**Keynes's summary of The General Theory (p. 245)** 1 Labour, capital, technology, and tastes are fixed His independent variables are • the marginal propensity to consume • the marginal efficiency of capital • the interest rate His dependent variables are • employment • output 2 The marginal propensity to consume, liquidity preference, and the marginal efficiency of capital determine employment and output (p. 247) Investment proceeds to the point where the marginal efficiency of capital equals the interest rate (p. 248) This is the summary of The General Theory (p. 249)
19	On the money wage Classical theory says that a wage reduction will reduce price and increase consumption, output, and employment. Keynes agrees (p. 258) But aggregate demand has to be considered (p. 260) Wage only affects employment if it alters the marginal propensity to consume, the marginal efficiency of capital, or the interest rate (p. 262) A wage reduction decreases the marginal propensity to consumer, but imports increase (p. 263) Changes in the money supply lead to changes in the wage (p. 268)
20	Employment is a function of consumption and investment Firms' profits are maximised when marginal revenue equals marginal cost (p. 283) Keynes sets out his cryptic view on maths
21	Highlights inconsistent claims that price is a function of demand and supply but that price is a function of the money supply (p. 292) Money is a link between present and future On methodology (p. 297) On maths (p. 298)
23	Mercantilism—the history of the argument that increased money supply lowers the interest rate Savings leads to poverty (p. 362ff)
24	The failures of the economy are the lack of full employment and inequality (p. 372) Keynes prefers a free market economy with full employment to socialism (p. 379) People don't heed any new theories after age 30! (p. 384)

Choice Quotes from Keynes's General Theory

'The propensity to consume and the rate of new investment determine between them the volume of employment' (p. 30)

'The decisions to consume and the decisions to invest between them determine incomes' (p. 64)

'Every such attempt to save more by reducing consumption will so affect incomes that the attempt necessarily defeats itself' (p. 84)

'the wage unit is, as a rule, the principal variable upon which the consumption-constituent of the aggregate demand function will depend' (p. 96)

'Consumption – to repeat the obvious – is the sole end and object of all economic activity. Opportunities for employment are necessarily limited by the extent of aggregate demand' (p. 104)

'We cannot, as a community, provide for future consumption by financial expedients, but only by current physical output' (p. 104)

'When the capital development of a country becomes a by-product of the activities of a casino, the job is likely to be ill-done' (p. 159)

'For my own part I am now somewhat sceptical of the success of a merely monetary policy directed towards influencing the rate of interest. I expect to see the State, which is in a position to calculate the marginal efficiency of capital-goods on long views and on the basis of the general social advantage, taking an ever greater responsibility for directly organising investment; since it seems likely that the fluctuations in the market estimation of the marginal efficiency of different types of capital, calculated on the principles I have described above, will be too great to be offset by any practicable changes in the rate of interest' (p. 164)

'It is evident then that the rate of interest is a highly psychological phenomenon' (p. 202)

'It might be more accurate perhaps to say that the rate of interest is a highly conventional, rather than a highly psychological phenomenon. For its actual value is largely governed by the prevailing view as to what its value is expected to be. *Any* level of interest which is accepted with sufficient conviction as *likely* to be durable, *will* be durable' (p. 203)

> 'Too large a proportion of recent "mathematical" economics are mere concoctions, as imprecise as the initial assumptions they rest on, which allow the author to lose sight of the complexities and interdependencies of the real world in a maze of pretentious and unhelpful symbols' (p. 298)
> 'I do not myself attach much value to manipulations of this kind....I doubt if they carry us any further than ordinary discourse can' (p. 305)
> 'I conceive therefore that a somewhat comprehensive socialisation of investment will prove the only means of securing an approximation to full employment' (p. 378)
> 'personal choice, the loss of which is the greatest of all losses of the homogenous or totalitarian state' (p. 380)

Reformulating Economics

A fundamental question is whether the economy is supply or demand led.

Whilst the famous simple supply and demand curve characterises popular concepts of economics, more philosophical attention to aggregate supply and demand is lacking. By definition, human survival depends on a minimum economic supply. Demand for necessities essential to life drives the economic production of supply, whether in hunting, farming, habitation, clothing, or energy. As the standard of living rises, again by definition, output demand and supply will be equal, unless stock building or withdrawal takes place. But as often happens in economics, the equality of demand and supply is post-hoc, i.e. after the event. Potential demand may well have been higher than supply if supply faced some limits or constraints. On the other hand, potential or actual supply may have exceeded demand, leaving idle production capacity, or unsold output, or unemployed labour. In more developed economies, a base level of demand is known and relatively stable. But as production technology becomes ever more efficient, the supply side of the economy is able to produce more goods and services than are needed to satisfy basic demand. Supply in this case initially exceeds demand, and has to create and enable demand to meet the increased supply output. Hence the need for advertising to present the goods and services available and to persuade consumers to purchase them. But the economic system also has to generate sufficient consumer income for consumers to be able to purchase the increased output. Wage is the traditional means relied on to supply consumer income, but is not always sufficient. Hence the development of credit to allow immediate purchase funded by future repayment from future wage. Credit cards are maxed out, HP contracts signed. Household debt then accumulates, whether unsecured, like the infamous pay day lending, or secured by extending mortgages and using the funds for consumption. Aggregate household debt mushrooms.

Once the supply side of an economy has become efficient with high levels of productivity, it's not unreasonable to see the process as supply led. Firms innovate and bring new products and services to market. Many of these have not been previously imagined by consumers, who have not expressed interest in their production, i.e. the process is not demand led, but supply led. The system then has to feed income to enable consumers to exert effective funded demand to match supply. As Keynes pointed out, in critique of Say's Law, supply does not necessarily create its own demand. If and when the system fails to generate sufficient consumer income, the crisis is one of demand, not of supply. The 2007 global economic crisis which began with the US 'sub-prime' mortgage market failure was a crisis of demand, not of supply. The supply side of the economy was well able to construct housing, and did. The demand side lacked sufficient income to buy the housing the supply side could readily construct. The debt taken out predictably proved unsustainable. New concepts of income beyond wage and debt are needed in high productivity economies.

A study and understanding of the sourcing and sufficiency of income in a dynamically growing economy, with high technology enabling huge leaps in productivity and therefore in output, is urgently needed. This is true whether in a context of economic growth, or if static or de-growth strategies are followed. Demand income deficiency results in all these cases from high productivity supply if and when wages are insufficient to fund effective demand. It's a key failing of the current economic system. It requires structural re-engineering of the economy.

Real Consumer Behaviour

The claim implicit in the infamous demand curve of entry level economics that consumers purchase according to the price of each commodity is simplistic, naïve, and untrue. The price of each product is one of very many variables which affect consumer purchase decisions. Neither will refuge in the claim of 'ceteris paribus' suffice. For a start, we need to distinguish between long-term and short term purchasing decisions, as well as between essential and discretionary purchases. Some purchases, for example of a house, a car, or consumer durables, are made in a long-term decision context, but carry forward expenditure obligations when they are funded by loans. Essential consumable purchases are also at least partially fixed obligations, meaning that their price will have little effect on their demand. The main effect of any increase in their price will be a so-called income effect, reducing the consumer's net disposable income available to buy other goods, and hence affecting demand for those other discretionary goods more than for the essential good itself. House prices will affect demand, but not necessarily to uniquely reduce demand for houses as their price rises. On the contrary, an initial rise in house prices may well generate consumer expectations that prices are set to rise further, and persuade some people to buy, thus increasing demand. This increased demand may either be for a long-term residence, with the decision to purchase driven by a desire to avoid expected higher future prices, or it may be driven by an element of speculation seeking to gain value as the house asset appreciates in value, or the purchase decision could be a combination of both these motivations. The speculative element of demand can easily become self-fulfilling, until the speculative bubble reaches the limits of its sustainability, or perhaps even bursts in a price crash. Consumers buying houses will also be affected by other prices, for example transaction costs, energy costs to service the house, and most importantly, mortgage costs. In general, mortgage interest rates will affect housing demand, but this again demonstrates that it is not only the price of the product itself which determines demand, but also the price of ancillary products, in this case the price of money, i.e. the interest rate. Since house purchase is a medium- to long-term purchase decision, consumers would ideally need to be informed of forward projection of these costs if they were to make a rational purchase decision. Future energy and mortgage interest prices are too uncertain and unknown for consumers to form rational expectations. In effect, consumers take a significant risk on these future costs. If energy and mortgage costs later reduce, then the consumer has increased net disposable income to spend on other discretionary purchases. But if these costs rise, consumers will suffer reduced net disposable income, and may reach a point where their mortgage payments become unaffordable, forcing them into default, and even into the repossession of the house by the lending bank. Their credit record may then prevent them from taking future loans, adding a regulatory/legal element to the consumer demand function. To make a rational purchase decision, the consumer would need to be able to forward guess not only interest rate movements resulting from money markets, but given the regular recourse to interest rate management of the economy by government, would need to be able to forward guess central bank monetary policy too. In fact government and central banks explicitly rely on interest rate manipulation in the misplaced hope of thereby managing the macroeconomy, partly by directly affecting the net disposable income of consumers holding house mortgages. All this suggests the advice of 'buyer beware'.

The price of housing in the rental market may affect demand more directly and immediately, but ultimately demand for housing will be fairly inelastic to price due to its necessity at some basic level. The price of housing, both housing to buy and to rent, will be driven by cost, but this cost will depend on political as well as economic variables. Housing costs will depend on construction, labour, raw material, and land cost, but the land cost itself will depend crucially on government political land use planning strategy.

Despite these myriad complications, consumers do buy houses. But they don't buy houses on a simple downward sloping demand curve. What actually happens is a mixture of informed rational decision, uninformed and therefore vague and often discounted future expectations, and entry into an iterative random process with unpredictable effects and outcomes.

Consumer demand will of course also depend on consumer income. Even this has finessed definitions, with Milton Friedman proposing permanent life-time income as the best determinant and explanation of consumer demand.

This iterative random process also characterises consumer demand for immediate discretionary consumables, far more than either the simple rational downward sloping price determined demand curve, or the complex inter-product indifference curves of mathematical academic microeconomics.

More research is needed on 'behavioural economics', set out by Michelle Baddeley in her 'Behavioural Economics: A Very Short Introduction'[13] which she characterises as 'a softer view of rationality' (p. 35). Consumers typically combine rational decision with a random walk which then has iterative effects. A distinction may be emerging between physical retail and online shopping. Online shopping offers wider product and price comparisons with immediate recalculation of the cumulative cost of a purchase basket. This may approach and more closely approximate to the model of 'perfect competition' too easily assumed in classic economic theory, which relies on perfect information. The consumer does now have the tools to switch purchases along supposed product indifference curves, but this still remains an unlikely or rare process. Consumers are unlikely to make real time comparisons of utility and price between products like tea or shampoo, certainly for minor price changes. More likely is that online purchasing resembles physical retail practice. Consumers begin their purchase basket, often with vague rather than accurate inter-product price awareness, and accumulate purchases to some point of assumed adequacy or to a budget constraint on total basket cost. Even this is only evident to most consumers at the check-out point, at which moment it is rare for consumers to reconsider their purchases. What might happen is that the consumer may later reevaluate their purchases, and decide next time to buy less or none of an expensive product, or to try a different supermarket for lower prices. This process is at best vague, intentional, and aspirational, rather than accurate, calculated, and rational. The more likely main effect is on net disposable income left after this purchase. Depending on the outcome of the first purchase action, consumers then find themselves with less left to spend on other purchases, either from their wage, pension, or benefit income, or due to their credit card limit. The time sequence with which the consumer makes purchases is important in determining which are the primary purchases, less constrained by considerations of price and income, and which become the secondary purchases where income constraints become more binding and price therefore more significant.

As well as understanding the nature of consumer purchasing practice, the factors determining demand for any one product are in any case wider than its price. Consumer appeal is affected by psychological mood, by powerful persuasive advertising, by image projection, by peer-group comparison, and by the launch of entirely new products and services.

Economics' assumption of 'rational agents' derives from Enlightenment thought, which established reason and logic as the true explanation of phenomena and the best basis for action. The Enlightenment project proved hugely successful and transformational in science, engineering, technology, medicine, and other spheres of the human experience. It also released humanity from dire fears derived from darker variants of religion and superstition, and led to an era of flourishing in the arts as well as in science. However, the unique supremacy of reason is challenged by the more holistic view of human nature which includes emotion. Economics insists that consumers exercise choice, but Enlightenment thinkers who emphasise causal understanding, and therefore take a deterministic view, such as the French philosopher André Comte-Sponville, claim that choice is a chimera, since if an event or phenomenon is caused, it cannot be considered as chosen. Consumer behaviour may indeed be as random as it is rational. In his 'Causality and Chance in Modern Physics',[14] the philosopher David Bohm explores the balance of rational and stochastic process, which he suggests changes with the level of perspective. For example, if we walk down the street during autumn, we may well regard a leaf falling on our head as a random event. But if we had access to more total system data, we may know that the level of sap in the leaf's stem, coupled with the shift in wind speed, would predict the fall of that specific leaf at that specific moment. If we were able to take even more of a 'helicopter view', we might be able to explain the leaf's level of sap, and the shift in the wind. The unanswered question is whether, from the perspective of a total overall view, everything is explained by causal reason, or an irreducible stochastic process exists in nature? The theory of evolution offers both rational-causal and random hypotheses. Darwin considered mutation to be a random process, and selection explained logically by the criterion of fitness,[15] whereas Lamarck explained mutation as a response to environmental causes.[16] Selection could also prove random, for example, if the antelope taken by the lion was simply unlucky to be found closest to the lion rather than being the least fit antelope to run. Returning to economics, some consumption has rational cause, but some may be simply random. A consumer may walk into a shop, see a product they had never previously considered, and buy it 'on impulse'. Impulse buying is a well-documented phenomenon, is regularly exploited by retailers who stack products next to check-out points, but is not recognised in economic theory. The random impulse purchase then reduces net disposable income, thus affecting onward consumer purchase. Meanwhile, the only space for a stochastic process in mainstream economics is in the error term of the least squares method of econometric regression equations.

Real consumer behaviour is therefore a combination of psychology, rationality, and a 'random walk' with an iterative process. Businesses supplying consumer markets know this and manage their marketing strategy accordingly. Academic economists have yet to realise that this is the real consumer process, and incorporate it in their microeconomic mathematical models and their macroeconomic consumption functions.

Real Firm Behaviour

Similarly real firms do not invest according to the interest rate, the price of money, or to the point where the marginal efficiency of capital equals this interest rate, or manufacture to the point where marginal revenue equals marginal cost. Only ivory tower academics can maintain and perpetuate such myths. Decisions to establish a firm, to diversify, to increase output and sales, will all take market product or service price into account, as well as the investment cost and its subsequent servicing costs. Careful consideration will be given to product specification, its demand for raw materials, its production process and labour requirement, its 'route to market' along a value chain, as well as to its proposed price. Consumer demand and competitive positioning will be carefully analysed in market research. All this will be analysed in the ubiquitous 'business plan' with a calculation of expected financial results, the rate of profit on sales revenues, and the rate of return on capital employed. Company management, shareholders, and lending banks will then make an investment decision against this business plan. The plan incorporates huge uncertainty, and so includes extensive risk analysis. Whilst the interest rate on any loan necessary to the venture will be analysed, the interest rate is only one of very many variables which are key to the plan's success. The cost of the capital investment, the product price and sales volume achievable, the cost of production, the risk of competitor response in lower prices or better products are all more important to the investment decision. Investment cannot in any case depend highly on the interest rate, because, whilst the current interest rate is known, the project may have a

20-year life, and 20-year forward projection of interest rates, particularly real interest rates after inflation, has a very wide confidence interval, too wide to be meaningful. Lending banks will impose their own criteria on their agreement to finance the investment. Apart from setting the interest rate and term for the loan with regular 'break points' requiring future refinancing, and charging an arrangement fee, banks typically require the lending business to demonstrate sufficient existing net assets to cover the loan, and sufficient current Earnings Before Interest, Taxes, Depreciation, and Amortisation (EBITDA) to cover interest payments on the loan, in the event that the new project fails to generate sufficient revenue or profit. In effect, banks are thereby only making investment funding available to existing businesses, and not to new businesses. This has a significant impact on economic growth. Banks have shifted all risk to the investing business, and imposed extensive conditionality which makes investment funding scarce. These realities mean that investment is subject to a very wide range of variables and constraints. Investment is not a simple function of interest rates, nor even only driven by expected future returns as Keynes claimed via his 'marginal efficiency of capital'.

The outcome of this process is that investments made against such business plans rarely achieve the business plan. Economies are dynamic. Sales may grow, platform, or decline, as may achievable price and therefore sales revenue. Costs, for example raw material and energy costs, may rise exogenously more than product price can be raised in its market, or new manufacturing technology, or outsourcing options, or economies of scale may reduce manufactured cost. Interest rates may go sky high. New products and services may sap demand. Effective business management is aware of these and other factors, and calibrates a strategic response. Some businesses might flourish way beyond expectations and report higher than expected profits, attracting high price/earnings ratios on stock markets. Or shareholders might take flight, whether rationally or psychologically, causing company valuation to drop, raising the threat of a takeover.

Once again, as with consumer behaviour, the real behaviour of firms is far more complex than simplistic economic theory of the firm allows. Firms' behaviour is again a combination of rational calculation, combined with optimal management of random processes and events. Profit is a requirement, but it is rarely a maximand. Investment and production are long-term processes which result from psychological, social, and political factors and are not simply subject to short term price alone. To understand the behaviour of firms more meaningfully in microeconomic theory of the firm, research would need to examine firm formation rates, firm failure rates, and the extent of conformity to or divergence from the firm's business plan. In the rational/random context firms face, they will seek to choose apparently optimal strategic actions, but monitor the results of these actions, and then continually adapt. They will equally monitor changes in external context, whether from customers, competitors, government, commercial banks, central banks, and stock markets, and again adapt as well as they can. The results could be good, bad, or indifferent, either because factors were well understood and responses well calibrated, or because internal or external random factors moved advantageously or to the firm's disadvantage. The phenomenon of large firms creates immense market power which can distort product and labour markets, as analysed in Di Mauro Mertens, and Mottironi 'Sources of large firms' market power and why it matters'.[17] These real-world processes are not captured in standard microeconomic models of the firm. Economic theory needs rewriting. A promising alternative methodology is in the growing field of experimental economics, as exemplified in the paper by Michael Webb 'The Impact of Artificial Intelligence on the Labor Market' (2020),[18] and in the papers reviewed in Gary Charness and Mark Pingle 'The Art of Experimental Economics - Twenty Top Papers Reviewed'[19] (2022).

References

1. Hal R. Varian, *Intermediate Microeconomics: A Modern Approach*, 9th ed. (New York: W.W. Norton & Company, 2014).
2. Charles I. Jones, *Macroeconomics*, 4th ed. (New York: W.W. Norton & Company, 2017).
3. Jonathan Levin and Paul Milgrom, 'Consumer Theory', October 2004, https://web.stanford.edu/~jdlevin/Econ%20202/Consumer%20Theory.pdf.
4. Massachusetts Institute of Technology, 'Principles of Microeconomics: Unit 2—Consumer Theory: Preferences and Utility', 2011, https://ocw.mit.edu/courses/14-01sc-principles-of-microeconomics-fall-2011/pages/unit-2-consumer-theory/preferences-and-utility/.
5. Milton Friedman, 'The Methodology of Positive Economics', in *Essays in Positive Economics* (Chicago: University of Chicago Press, 1966), 3–16, 30–43.

6. George H. Blackford, 'On the Pseudo-Scientific Nature of Friedman's "as If" Methodology', 2017 www.rweconomics.com/BPA.htm.
7. Stewart Shapiro, *Thinking About Mathematics: The Philosophy of Mathematics* (Oxford: Oxford University Press, 2000).
8. Leonid V. Kantorovich, 'Mathematical Methods of Organizing and Planning Production', *Management Science* 6, no. 4 (1960): 366–422.
9. The Nobel Prize, 'The Sveriges Riksbank Prize in Economic Sciences in Memory of Alfred Nobel 1975: Leonid Kantorovich and Tjalling Koopmans', 1975, www.nobelprize.org/prizes/economic-sciences/1975/kantorovich/biographical/.
10. George B. Dantzig, 'Maximization of a Linear Function of Variables Subject to Linear Inequalities', in *Activity Analysis of Production and Allocation*, ed. T. C. Koopmans (John Wiley & Sons, 1947).
11. Gottlob Frege, *The Foundations of Arithmetic (Die Grundlagen Der Arithmetik)* (Oxford: Basil Blackwell, 1884).
12. Axel Leijonhufvud, *On Keynesian Economics and the Economics of Keynes* (New York: Oxford University Press, 1968).
13. Michelle Baddeley, *Behavioural Economics: A Very Short Introduction* (Oxford: Oxford University Press, 2017).
14. David Bohm, *Causality and Chance in Modern Physics* (London: Routledge & Kegan Paul, 1957).
15. Charles Darwin, *On the Origin of Species* (London: John Murray, 1859).
16. Jean-Baptiste Lamarck, *Philosophie Zoologique* (Paris: Dentu, 1809).
17. VoxEU Centre for Economic Policy Research, 'The Sources of Large Firms' Market Power and Why It Matters', 2024, https://cepr.org/voxeu/columns/sources-large-firms-market-power-and-why-it-matters.
18. Michael Webb, *The Impact of Artificial Intelligence on the Labor Market* (Stanford University, January 2020), www.michaelwebb.co/webb_ai.pdf.
19. Gary Charness and Mark Pingle, *The Art of Experimental Economics: Twenty Top Papers Reviewed* (London: Routledge, 2021).

Index

A
austerity, v, 4, 55, 62, 66, 105, 111
automation, vi, 2, 4, 8, 31, 33, 39, 51, 72–79, 81–83, 88, 95, 107

B
behavioural economics, 122

C
Cambridge Econometrics, 2, 39, 40
conditionality, vi, 3, 39, 40, 51, 96, 125

D
debt/GDP, 3, 52, 63, 66, 105
direct money financing, vi, 3, 4, 39, 40, 44, 46, 59–62, 65–67, 96

E
economies of scale, 2, 72–75, 125
experimental economics, 78, 126

F
financial crisis, 20, 37
Friedman, Milton, 50, 106, 121

G
government debt, 3, 4, 30, 55–59, 61, 62, 67, 96, 111, 113

H
household debt, 8, 19, 21–28, 73, 84, 105, 119
household income, v, 2, 8–13, 18, 28, 29, 32, 36, 37, 74, 75, 84, 95, 96

I
inequality, v, 8, 11–13, 32, 38, 56, 73, 78–81, 83, 105, 111, 116
inflation, 50, 51, 55, 57, 60, 62, 66, 101, 102, 106, 114, 125
Institute for Policy Research, 2, 23–28, 40

INDEX

interest rate, 46, 50, 51, 55–58, 60, 66, 88, 101, 102, 105, 106, 111, 112, 115, 116, 120, 124

K

Keynesian, 1, 50, 62, 105, 112, 113
Keynes, John Maynard, 1, 3, 29, 31, 46, 52, 66, 101, 104, 105, 109, 111–117, 119, 125

L

labour augmentation, 75
labour displacement, 73, 75, 77
labour share, 2, 8, 24, 28, 31, 32, 72, 73, 75, 77–81, 83, 84, 88, 95, 105
Leijonhufvud, Axel, 1, 113

M

magic money tree, 46
mathematics, 108–110
minimum wage, 33–35, 38
Modern Monetary Theory, 3, 63
monetary policy, 3, 44, 50, 63
money, v, vi, 3, 4, 30, 33, 39, 40, 44–46, 50–52, 55, 59–63, 65–67, 86, 95, 96, 101, 102, 105, 111, 112, 114–116, 120, 124

N

neoclassical economics, 101

P

pensions, 18, 29
policy, vi, 3, 4, 8, 28, 30, 33, 40, 44–46, 50, 51, 55, 59–63, 66, 74, 80, 82, 83, 87, 89, 95, 98, 102, 104, 106, 110–112, 115, 117, 121
poverty, v, 1–3, 9, 28, 32, 38–40, 73, 83, 88, 98, 105, 111, 116
price, vi, 2, 30, 45, 50, 58, 60, 66, 72, 74–77, 84, 88, 98–105, 107, 108, 110, 111, 113–116, 120–122, 124, 125
productivity, 30, 31, 51, 72, 78, 80–82, 85–88, 96, 104–106, 110, 115, 119

Q

quantitative easing (QE), 3, 44, 55–62, 64, 66, 67
quantitative tightening, 3

S

seigniorage, 45, 52, 62, 105
Solow, Robert, 2, 81, 85

T

technology, vi, 1, 2, 4, 8, 31–33, 39, 55, 72–76, 78, 80, 81, 83–89, 96, 99, 102, 106, 108, 111–113, 115, 116, 118, 119, 123, 125

U

universal basic income (UBI), 2, 30, 73, 79–82

W

welfare benefits, 3, 8, 9, 30, 36, 38–40, 73, 84, 105
work, 29–31, 80, 82, 83

The manufacturer's authorised representative in the EU is Springer Nature Customer Service Centre GmbH, Europaplatz 3, 69115 Heidelberg, Germany. If you have any concerns regarding our products, please contact ProductSafety@springernature.com

Printed and bound by CPI Group (UK) Ltd, Croydon, CR0 4YY
13/10/2025
01974698-0001